Cut From The
Wilderness

Cut From The
Wilderness

The True Story of an Alaskan Homestead Girl

Alicia Loveland

PO Box 221974 Anchorage, Alaska 99522-1974
books@publicationconsultants.com—www.publicationconsultants.com

ISBN 978-1-59433-236-4
Library of Congress Catalog Card Number: 2011927972

Manufactured in the United States of America.

It's the great, big broad land way up yonder

It's the forest where silence has lease

It's the beauty that thrills me with wonder

It's the stillness that fills me with peace

By Robert Service

I dedicate this book

posthumously to my

grandpa Pete and

my brother Dave for

being my heroes.

Acknowledgments

I WANTED TO WRITE THIS BOOK MANY YEARS AGO BUT I PUT IT OFF because it seemed so overwhelming until my friends, Susan and Bernd Richter urged me on. Thank you to them for their encouragement and support. I also want to thank my friends, Karen Henneck for pushing me to write more details and supporting me through the project. A thank you also goes to Betty Gosar for proof reading, and George Rogers for reading the manuscript and giving suggestions. A thank you and a big kiss go to my husband for his help and support.

Contents

The old cache before we took it down.

Introduction

SIXTY-TWO YEARS OLD AND HERE I AM, PEELING BLACK SPRUCE LOGS again. I jerk the draw blade down the dry tree and it only gives up a small strip of bark. It never was easy peeling logs, but when I was twelve, the logs seemed to give up more bark with each swipe of the blade. I only need four twelve foot logs for the new deck Ron, my husband, is putting on the old cache but it is taking me forever. Part of my problem is that I look at the cache with its sagging, wooden- shingled roof, age-darkened logs, and rotten deck and I find myself daydreaming about its grander days fifty years ago. A 2x4 latches the door closed and an old piece of caribou horn passes for a handle on the heavy, split- log door.

My mind wanders back in time and I see the cache when Dad built it on our homestead. It was a grand little cabin sitting on top of its log poles high in the air. We used it to store our caribou and moose away from the bears and in the summer when all of the meat was gone, I slept in it. I also used it to get away from everyone when I wanted to be alone. When it tipped precariously on its rotting logs, we hired someone to hold it up with a forklift while my husband and son cut off as much of the poles as they could with the chainsaw. With my heart in my throat, I watched this old piece of history sway and lurch across the road and down the driveway onto our piece of the homestead atop the forklift.

Transporting the cache across the road to our side of the homestead.

The old cache became a cabin.

The cache means so much to me because of my history with it that I breathed a sigh of relief when the driver set it down in the tundra beside our cabin. Once on the ground, it sat lopsided because of the log poles all being cut off at different lengths. Dad put the 55-gallon gasoline half- barrels over the tops of the poles to keep squirrels out of the cache. The barrels had to sit squarely on the ground under the cache or it would always be at a tilt. Ron jacked the cabin up on each side with the only jacks we had. They were two small handy- man jacks not meant for such a big job. I had to cut these poles off under the corner barrels and it terrified me to reach under each jagged- edged barrel and cut through the log with a Sawsall. I knew that if one of the jacks fell over and the cabin fell, the barrel would cut my arm off. I slowly cut through each log holding my breath with each agonizing minute.

Now the 10x12 cache sits squarely on the barrels and restoration has begun. I conjure up pictures of the cache on our family homestead as I strip away the bark on the log. Pictures are like windows looking into the past. They bring the memories forward and I find myself drifting back to a time when I first came to Cantwell, Alaska.

CHAPTER I

1954

fall to fall

MOM TOOK ME TO THE ANCHORAGE RAILROAD STATION AT THE
bottom of 3rd Street and put me on the train August 11. She handed
a man with a black uniform and black hat my ticket and told him I
was travelling alone and then waved at me until I could no longer see
her. At the age of eight, it was an adventure riding the train for the
first time. I felt grown up doing it on my own, but at the same time,
it was scary travelling alone. I was going to visit my Grandparents in
Cantwell, Alaska.

The train chugged its way over the tracks. I didn't bother to look at
the scenery outside; my whole attention wrapped around the people I
saw in my rail car. There were mostly grizzly young and old men with
beards. A few women sat across the aisle knitting or reading a book.
Two kids sat farther down the aisle staring idly out the window.

It seemed like hours as the train lumbered along and I wanted to do
something to break the monotony. I didn't know if I was allowed to get
up and explore so I just sat, hour after hour. Finally, I dozed off out of
boredom and drifted in and out of sleep as we stopped at one station
after another. Then, we slowed and people put on their coats. I sat up
fully awake.

The train screeched to a stop at Curry, a small rail community next
to the Susitna River. A wide, wooden plank platform went from the

train right up to the door of an old hotel. This was the old Curry Hotel built in 1923 for railroad passengers when it took three days and two nights to get from Seward to Fairbanks.

Surprised to see the big hotel sitting there in the middle of nowhere, I asked a woman in the seat across the aisle, "What are we doing?"

People got off and walked into the hotel but I didn't think this was the town where I was supposed to be getting off. The woman smiled and replied, "We're taking on water from that big water tank over there. You can get off if you'd like because we're going to be here for awhile."

I followed behind her into the hotel lobby with the others. Huge leather chairs with metal bottoms sat in the lobby and they all filled with train passengers. I bought a dozen old chocolate- covered marshmallow eggs from Easter and climbed back onto the train, afraid that I might miss getting on if it pulled out. Then I settled down to eat the whole dozen. They were as tough as nails but I gnawed through them anyway. After what seemed like a long time, the train whistle blew, people scampered across the platform onto the train and the churning metal wheels grabbed the rail as we slowly crept forward until we picked up our speed again.

This time, I took more interest in the scenery as I looked out the large train windows at the passing fall-colored trees. As the train travelled down the tracks, people migrated from car to car to see if they knew anyone since this was the mode of transportation for many of the Interior Alaskan people. Roads were sparse and the rail was the only way to get to these small communities. The train stopped at every fishing hole because someone flagged us down to get on or someone wanted to get off. The farther north we traveled, the redder the salmon were in the streams next to the tracks. They laid their eggs and were ready to die. The long swim from the ocean up the fresh water rivers and streams to this point rotted their bodies. Bored with watching the swarming fish in the side waters of the streams, I headed for the dining car to eat lunch.

When I asked the conductor about moving around, he said, "Sure, you can go anyplace you want on this train."

I hadn't eaten since 8 AM and I was hungry. I sat at a table by myself and self- consciously waited for the waiter. When the waiter came, he took my order and as he left my table, he spread his legs to keep his balance and grabbed onto the side of my table. As the train rocked side to side, people apologized to seated passengers for lurching forward or stumbling backwards into the tables. If the train made a stop for anglers, the wheels made a screeching sound and everyone swayed forward as the train came to a stop. Eating was difficult because of the train motion but I managed to eat a toasted cheese sandwich and drink a soda without making a mess. I sat, mesmerized, as my Coke walked its way across the slick tablecloth stopping short of falling off the edge.

Passengers pressed their noses to the windows and they all talked at once.

"Look at that!"

"Oh my gosh!"

'That looks like a long way down!"

I pressed my nose to the window to see what they were talking about just as we passed over a long trestle. Way down at the bottom of the ravine a small river wound its way through the gulch. The trestle crossed over Hurricane Gulch. This trestle measured 918 feet across and it was 296 feet down to the bottom of the gulch. I watched, fascinated but scared as we slowly crossed over. I searched the faces of those around me for reassurance that the trail wouldn't derail. The train slowed considerably as we crossed the trestle and I didn't know whether we slowed because they thought the heavy train might fall through the trestle or they were letting everyone see the deep gulch.

Soon, the conductor walked through the dining car and announced, "Summit. Next stop."

He stopped in front of me and said, "You need to go back to your seat little lady because the stop after Summit is Cantwell."

I handed the waiter my five -dollar bill and he handed me change before I hurried down the aisle through one car after another to my seat. The fresh air between cars felt good on my face.

As I stepped off the train in Cantwell, I looked around at the old buildings sitting close by. A small, square, gray building sat on railroad ties beside the tracks. A sign over the door read POST OFFICE. Four wide wooden steps led up to a broad porch deck. Some of the people milling around the base of the steps smiled at me and nodded as though they knew me. They all waited for the mailbag to be brought in by the railroad cargo man and then for the postmistress to sort the mail. Over the years, I recognized that this spot on the steps or on the deck was the social place in the community. While people waited for the train, they stood at this location visiting with neighbors and exchanging news.

A little farther north, across a small bridge, sat a green one-story railroad section house used to house the railroad extra-gang who worked on the tracks and the railroad station manager, Jonsie.

After the cargo man handed down my small suitcase from the cargo car, I collected it and stood beside the tracks waiting for Grandma as the train pulled away. When she arrived, she hugged me and then loaded my suitcase into the trunk of the car. She informed me that we needed to stop at the store before we went home. Grandma looked the same as she had two years previously with her short, light brown hair but she had grayed a little at the temples. Her gold wire rimmed glasses set off her pretty face. She always appeared a little nervous and filled with energy. The store she said we needed to go to sat on the other side of a wide patch of gravel and when I looked ahead to see where we were going, I saw a big sign with bold black letters reading CARLSON'S ROADHOUSE AND STORE above the door of an old cabin. Inside were sagging shelves of grocery items in one room of the cabin. Jack West, the owner, used the other room as a visiting/living area. A fire burned in a barrel stove sitting in the living area. Local men drew up their chairs and poured steaming coffee from the metal coffee pot that always sat on top of the stove. I can't remember a time when men weren't sitting around the stove. I remember going in to buy things over the years and listing the items in a book marked "On Account" sitting on the counter. Most of the time, Mr. West didn't even go into the grocery area unless he wanted to talk to the customer. He trusted everyone to write his or her items down. Customers only paid their bill once a month.

Jack West, the owner, greeted us at the door that day. He started out as John Carlson's silent partner for the store in 1919. He was a trapper by trade and that enabled him to continue trapping. He gave up his trapping and took over the store when Carlson died in 1932.

Mr. West wore faded red suspenders and a long-sleeved wool shirt the day I met him. He usually wore that same attire every day over the years. About half of the time, he left off the shirt and wore the suspenders over his long white underwear. A bit of chewing tobacco juice dribbled from the corner of his mouth from chewing and spitting. He seemed very old and harsh with his white whiskered stubble as he shuffled around the room but I grew very fond of him over the years. He always took time to talk to me and ask if I would like to see his gold nuggets. The large nuggets in his jar were very impressive and I loved hearing him tell stories about the gold miners.

When I visited the store over the years, I listened to the men's stories in the smoke-filled little room. They were all comfortable with each other as they rambled on and on with one story after another.

"Remember that old guy who came out of the mountains with all that rich ore?"

"Yeah, what was his name anyway?"

"I don't know. I just remember that ore in his pack. It was damned good lookin stuff."

"Too bad he couldn't find that place again after he had his ore assayed."

"Yeah, well those mountains all look alike and when you get in that underbrush, you can't see anything."

"I never saw him again. I heard he never found the place again."

After Grandma and I collected the groceries that first day, we left the cabins of Cantwell and drove down a gravel road leading east with rocks spitting out from under our tires. Around a wide curve, I spotted a small grouping of about six small log cabins to our left.

"What's that Grandma?" I asked.

"It's the Native village."

Cantwell village in 1954.

"How many people live in Cantwell?"

"There are about eighty plus."

"How many are Native?"

"About forty"

After passing the cabins, we crossed Jack River via a wooden bridge and continued for about another mile past a few more cabins and on to the Alaska Road Commission property and my grandparent's house. It was a two story, gray, shake-sided house where I had my own bedroom. In the first hour, I discovered the greatest thing about this house and that was a laundry chute from the upstairs to the empty basement floor. I dropped a towel down the chute to watch it slide to the concrete floor below.

Kids lived nearby and within a day, I was playing with my seven-year-old Uncle Peter, neighboring kids and a boy named Charlie. Grandma took care of Charlie in the daytime while his dad worked at the Road Commission. Charlie's dad had custody of him for the summer. I made new friends and I made another kind of friend at the same time.

Grandma had a cocker spaniel named Tiny. Right from the beginning, we were friends. When I fed him his Skippy food in the evening,

I ate a teaspoonful as well. "Here Tiny. Here is one for you and one for me." My way of making him feel that we were friends was by sharing his meal with him. I stopped eating the dog food when I found a screw mixed in with the canned dog food. One day a passing dump truck hit him and I lost my little friend. Grandma had had Tiny since she lived in Anchorage and now she had no pet and I had no furry friend.

———————————————|■|———————————————

Grandpa and Grandma moved to Cantwell in 1952 when Grandpa became the General Foreman for the Cantwell Alaska Road Commission Camp. They built the road from Cantwell to Paxson (now called the Denali Highway). This 133 mile, rough, gravel road, washed out often and lay riddled with potholes and rough shards of rock. Surprisingly, it is still the same all these years later. They completed the road in 1958. They also built the 28 mile road from Cantwell to McKinley National Park, (now called Denali Park) and a 10-mile stretch from Cantwell to Summit, a pre WWII Civil Aeronautics site that later became an FAA station. Grandpa told me that he sent one of the Natives out on a D-8 Cat toward Paxson. He told John to "find a road" (they followed many trails in those days to build roads), and the man followed a trail only to lose the Cat deep in the bog. Grandpa said, "It wasn't an easy road to put in, but then, none of the roads in Alaska were easy with the mosquitoes, mud, bog, rivers, brush and forests." They built a bridge on the Denali Highway in the winter to use the ice as their work platform. It would have been too difficult to build the bridge with water rushing down the river. When the ice melted in the spring, the bridge was finished.

Grandpa was no newcomer to building roads. He shared history of his road building adventures with his friends in the evenings and I listened. "I helped build the Wonder Lake Road in McKinley Park from 1927 to 1937 and went on to build the roads at Illiamna and Homer after that. When my boss directed me to build the road from Anchorage to the Canadian border at the start of WW II, I told him I didn't want the job because I was burned out. My boss told me I could do it with them or do it with the Army since they would draft me into the Sea-Bees. While there, I would have to build the roads under enemy fire on Attu Island or Kiska. I accepted his assignment and moved to Sutton where I hired whoever came along: drunks, draft dodgers, and rejects since the draft took everyone else. In the summer, I hired young boys and taught them how to use the equipment. They worked out great and in 1946, we completed the road. I went on to build roads in the Palmer, Kodiak, Naknek, Dillingham, Takotna, Flat and Talkeetna areas in Alaska. " For Grandpa's whole life, until he retired, he moved around building one road after another.

The start of the Alcan Highway through Canada in the 1940s.

He didn't just talk about his road building though. He talked about the history of Cantwell as well. He said that earlier gold mining took place seventy miles east of Cantwell at Valdez Creek (once called Denali), and he told me of the Cantwell reindeer herding that took place in the 1920s. I loved history and soon my Cantwell history turned to world history in school.

I started school in a single-windowed, one-room Quonset hut that year with the teachers Mr. and Mrs. Woodall. The Quonset was dismal with the single window at each end. When the generator shut down, our lights went out, and we sat quietly waiting in the near-dark room for the return of lights. The generator for the lights came on in a short time since the Road Commission people also sat in the dark. In those days, people owned their own generator for electricity, tied into the Road Commissions generator if they were an employee, or they went without electricity. Some days, it wasn't the lights going out, it was our little stove. When the oil stove went out, the room chilled down quickly and sometimes it took all day to get the stove up and running again. We went home shortly after the stove shut down on those days. In a cold schoolroom there was no activity to keep our blood flowing but with no playground equipment for recesses, we wrestled with each other or chased each other around the gravel yard to stay warm.

Cantwell in 1936.

Halloween came and Grandma drove Peter and me to the store. I discovered the generosity of Jack West. He gave a full box of candy to each kid as we lined up and went through the door. We stood outside the small store stomping our feet in the crunchy snow just to stay warm as we giggled with excitement We didn't have store- bought costumes and kids who couldn't think of anything to put on as a costume only had a brown paper bag with cut out holes to see for their costume. Some even tried to go through the line twice, but Mr. West laughed and said, "I think I've seen you before." Since Cantwell didn't have many residents and people were scattered in the Native village cabins, fur trapper cabins, Road Commission worker cabins and a few miscellaneous cabins, the store was the only place to go trick or treating. I discovered that a few of the store's candy bars had mouse droppings in the box and worms in the Baby Ruth nuts over the years. They had been on the shelves for some time but continued to sell two candy bars for twenty-five cents. The store didn't carry my favorite candies which were bacon strips (sugar candy with bands of different colors), Neccos, or black licorice, but I loved getting whatever Mr. West had if it had sugar in it. Halloween was a treat but the next day held an even bigger treat.

On November 1, my mom came to Cantwell and hid in the closet before I came home from school. Peter bugged me saying, "Look in the closet! Look in the closet!" and when I finally did, Mom jumped out. She brought Halloween candy, a costume (too late), and a big teddy bear. I was thrilled to see her and to hear that she would be sharing my bedroom with me. Having Mom's undivided attention was nice but it didn't last long enough.

Two nights after Mom arrived in Cantwell, Charlie's father Everett, a parts warehouseman, came to visit Grandpa and meet the pretty, new woman in town, but he left Mom unimpressed. This slim, 5'10" man wore a leather coat with fringe hanging off the sleeves. He had laughing eyes, a boyish grin, and side-parted black hair with a curl coming down over one side of his forehead. When tickled over something, he laughed, his eyes crinkled and he slapped his knee. She just didn't care for him on that initial meeting so she went into the bedroom and Everett visited with Grandpa for the evening. Everett didn't give up. Mom was a slender, beautiful woman with long chestnut hair, high cheekbones and a beguiling smile. Men melted into little boys around her. At some point, Everett must have appeared differently to her because within a week, she saw him every evening. They even went snowshoeing even though she wasn't an outdoor person. One night,

My Mom when she came
to Cantwell in 1954.

six weeks later; she asked me, "How do you feel about having a new
daddy?" I said I wouldn't mind and on December 20, they left for
South Dakota, where his parents lived, to get married. They had a short
honeymoon before their return.

When they returned, they found a little dog for me. I named him
Tippy because of his black body with white tips on his feet and tail.
We moved into a small trailer and lean-to tucked back in the trees
next to the graveled, Denali Highway and Mom and Dad fixed up the
trailer with its two bedrooms, bathroom, kitchen and dining area and
living room lean-to with what little money they had that first winter.
They built end tables, a built-in couch, wood lamp bases, shelves, and
wooden valances out of 2x4s and plywood. Then they painted ivy on
the end wall and made curtains and throw pillows, which made the
lean-to very homey. Only plain painted plywood covered the floor but
the room looked very cozy. Mom was so into painting that I left a note
for Dad one day saying,

Dear Daddy,
Tell Mama that the door is scratched because I, for the fun
of it, locked Tippy in. Please forgive me for my meanness.
Since Mom likes to paint, she can paint it. From Alicia.

Tippy followed me everywhere and even went to school a half a block away to wait for me in the afternoon. One day he didn't meet me after school. I called and searched for him everywhere but I couldn't find him. When I went to Mom and asked if she had seen him, she said, "Someone must have picked him up." Every day I waited for him to come back, but he didn't. After this went on for a while, Mom confessed that Dad shot him. She didn't really give an explanation. I think they thought of him as a nuisance because of his puppy exuberance. I hated the way people disposed of animals so easily, especially one that I loved.

It made me think of a story Grandpa told me about a cat Mom and my aunt had as children. One day in January, the cat jumped on the table, licked the frosting off a newly baked cake of Grandma's, and then jumped in my aunt's face, scratching her. Grandpa didn't tolerate animals that didn't behave so he took the cat out to dispose of it. He put it in a gunnysack, threw it in the river and shot holes in the bag. In April, three months later, the cat came back with streaks of hairless areas on its body. They couldn't believe that this could be the same cat until he went to the exact spot where his water bowl had been. Grandpa let the cat stay for a while longer before getting rid of him for good.

In those days, people didn't keep an animal around if they felt the animal was worthless and I cried every time I heard of an animal suffering or lost a pet.

Concentrating on my own studies at school was difficult because there were seventeen of us from grades one through eight in the same room. When the teacher asked another student in a higher grade a question, my hand shot up to answer. On several occasions, the teacher chastised me with, "Study your books. You're not supposed to be listening to us." The upper grade seemed more interesting and the teacher finally let me be a part of that grade.

Sometimes, when the teacher's attention was elsewhere, we passed

Grandpa living in a small trailer working on one of the roads in 1954.

notes or wrote notes on our hands. When she caught us with these hand notes, we had to wash in front of the other kids while they giggled behind their hands. We went to the front of the room and pumped water from the well into the metal washbasin to wash. I only did it once to learn my lesson. Grandpa always had stories about lessons learned or how it was in his day and I realized that my trials weren't the end of the world.

Grandpa spent time with me those first few years in Cantwell because Grandma and my Uncle Peter moved back to Anchorage for Peter to go to school in a larger school and to take care of my great grandma on my grandma's side. I loved being around Grandpa because he either told stories or sang songs with his nice baritone voice. He burst out in song at the drop of a hat. After having a few drinks on weekends, while he lived the bachelor life, he recited poetry, sang songs, or told stories about people he knew. He said, "Mitme (his name for me), I'm going to teach you a poem." And off he would go. When he told stories, everyone laughed. He told one story about a story told to him by Paddy McCafferty, an old railroad man. Paddy told him about a prospector who froze to death on the trail between Cantwell and Valdez Creek. The man froze lying on his side with his legs at an eighty-degree angle and his shoulders pulled forward. They needed to get him into a box to go on the train and because of his frozen angle, he didn't fit, so Paddy laid the frozen man on his back and strapped his shoulders and legs down. They built a fire in the little hut beside the tracks to thaw the prospector out, but when one of the Nicklie men came to wait for the train in the hut, Paddy couldn't resist a practical joke. He cut the strap on the dead man's legs and when the legs shot up in the air, Mr. Nicklie shot out of the hut as if he had seen a ghost. Grandpa laughed over that story for years. Grandpa was outright funny with his stories but I was unintentionally funny.

I always said things in innocence that made people laugh. One day, the teacher said, "I want each of you to stand and tell what nationality your fathers are." The majority of the kids were Alaskan Athabaskan Natives so each of them stood up and said their fathers were Athabaskans.

When my turn came, I stood up and said, "My father is Bohunk." That is what I had heard others call Dad because his parents were Bohemian. Well, all the kids laughed because they had never heard the term. Overcome with indignation, I spouted, "He's just as good as any white man!" When my dad heard about it, he laughed until he cried. He explained a little about his family and their customs.

"My grandparents on my mother's side raised twelve children on a farm in South Dakota. For thirty miles around them, fifty percent were Bohemians from Czechoslovakia. After all the kids were born, Dad's grandfather died. A short time later, my grandfather's brother came from Czechoslovakia to marry his brother's widow following the custom of their country. Fortunately, the brother was a kind man, had a good sense of humor, and everyone loved him." Dad never did explain why they called them Bohunks.

CHAPTER 2

1955

fall to fall

AFTER OUR YEAR IN THE QUONSET, ALL OF US KIDS MOVED TO A one-room schoolhouse with a big bay window housing three panels of six small glass panes in each. There were high windows on the opposite wall as well, which made it a brighter room. They named our new little school the Golden Rule School. Grandpa played a major role in our having that school. My family's history included that building since Mom and my aunt went to that same schoolhouse as children in McKinley Park. The Cantwell acquisition of that school started with Grandpa's road building.

In 1927, Grandpa helped build the road from the Park entrance to Wonder Lake (a lake about eighty-five miles into the park). I listened to his story of how hard life was. "We lived with primitive accommodations in leaky World War I surplus tents. The floors were mud and the army cots had straw mattresses. We usually had good food, but one cook was an exception. We called him Dysentery Denny. I do not have to tell you what kind of food he cooked. The others had names like Happy Jack, Brown Gravy George, Mulligan Louie, and one-armed Joe. These cooks fed twenty to thirty men in the roughest of

Grandma and Grandpa in 1933.

Grandpa at Kantishna in McKinley Park when they were building the road to Wonder Lake.

The cabin my grandparents owned in McKinley Park.

conditions. The cooks slipped on the mud floors as they waded across with rubber boots, and slid between the stove and the 2x12x8-foot planks that served as tables. If we were lucky, we bathed once a week in the bath tent, but if we were on the move, we didn't bathe at all."

The park was only open seasonally from March 1 to November 1 in those days and Grandpa was fortunate enough to work year round. He stayed at the McKinley Park Station overhauling equipment. Appropriations came from Washington and sometimes they ran out of money so everyone went home. Grandpa recalled, "Wages were $4.50 a day with room and board and work hours were from 'now till then', sometimes sixteen hours a day."

In 1934, he bought a cabin from a man named Les Plumb for $175. Mom, age five; my aunt Babe, age four; Grandma and he moved into the cabin in McKinley Park. It was a one-room 16x24 cabin with a sod roof and partitioned off on the inside with a sheet draped over a wire to make two bedrooms. Grandpa said their furnishings were sparse at best. My mom recalled, "We hauled all of our water up a hill. We used kerosene lanterns and the cabin was always dark. Grandma did the laundry by hand on a scrub board and she sawed the wood for the stove with a big cross saw while your aunt and I sat on the log in the log holder to anchor it."

Grandpa's friend, Maurice Moreno, had a roadhouse close to the railroad tracks about a mile up the road. People bought supplies from him and picked up their mail since Moreno's place housed a post office, grocery store, and roadhouse. This two-story log building had twelve rooms, a dining room and lunch counter. There were also two apartments, which they called the chicken house. The whole building had log rails on the upper and lower levels and looked typically Alaskan.

Everyone was broke in those days and so for Christmas, they all chipped in and bought a keg of Totem beer from the Fairbanks brewery, pop and candy for the kids, and some toys. There were only six kids, seven men, five women and two park rangers there at that time.

At Easter, the parents hid Easter eggs for the kids, which consisted of my mom, aunt, the Lottsfelt kids, and two other kids. The Lottsfelt kids, whose father worked for the McKinley Park Service, owned horses and my aunt remembers the kids trying to swim in the horse's trough.

Moreno's roadhouse/store/post office in McKinley Park during the 1930s.

One time when Grandpa and Grandpa were gone, my aunt started a fire in the wood box just to see if it would burn. Fortunately, it didn't burn long before going out. Another time when they were alone, they left the cabin to find Grandma and Grandpa because they were scared. Somehow, they became lost in the woods and wandered around in deep snow for several hours before finally seeing smoke from their own cabin chimney to lead them back home.

Grandma canned moose meat in fruit jars for the whole year. She also made root beer in a big, galvanized tub, then jugged it up in milk bottles and capped it with rubber caps. She, my mom and aunt picked blueberries in that same galvanized tub and lugged it back to the cabin.

Their first outhouse was just a fallen log to sit on with a canvas mounted in front. When the wolves howled at night Mom was terrified to go outside. She and my aunt dreaded having to dump the honey bucket in the outhouse at night. Mom also dreaded another

Mom, my aunt and the Lottsfelt kids in McKinley Park having an Easter egg hunt in 1934.

experience with the honey bucket. Grandpa put Mom's fingers in the honey bucket to break her of chewing her fingernails. From then on, she chewed the skin on her knuckles.

Another outhouse memory involved a neighbor and my mother. Only one short road ran from the railroad station to the ranger station and one time four-year-old Buzz Lottsfelt, who was mad at his parents, made it all the way down the road from the ranger station and up the wooded hill to Grandpa's cabin, which was better than a mile or two away. He and Mom hid in the new outhouse and it tipped over and went all the way down the hill with them in it.

In 1937, my mom and aunt went to school in the railroad depot but Grandma decided they needed to go to school in Anchorage after that year because they couldn't find a teacher to come and teach so few kids. That's when Grandma, Aunt Babe and Mom moved back to Anchorage. Grandpa sold the cabin to Mr. Giglioni and went on to Colorado Station to build twelve miles of road into the Golden Zone gold mine, about thirty to forty miles from Cantwell.

The Alaska Railroad depot/school where Mom and my aunt went to school. It was the same building they used in Cantwell where I went to school.

The park no longer needed the little, old railroad depot/schoolhouse where Mom and my aunt went, so Grandpa decided it would be a marked improvement over the Quonset hut we used my first year. He requisitioned it for Cantwell. They took off the existing porch entrance to make it easier to move and hauled it to the railroad trestle. The building was too tall to go under the trestle so they put it in the river to float it across and when it got away from them, it slipped away and floated down the river. They snagged it, dragged it back up the river and pulled it across.

Our teacher placed a horseshoe above the door of the little building, and named it The Golden Rule School. The only connection we had with the Quonset after that was if we did something to make my fourth grade teacher mad. The offenders were banished to the Quonset hut next door to sit in the dark for however long it took the teacher to forgive them. Sometimes hours passed before we saw their faces again.

The Golden Rule School in Cantwell that at one time was the McKinley Park depot/school where Mom and my aunt went to school. The building beside it is the Quonset hut where I went to school in the third grade.

We had daily hygiene inspections by the teacher. I remember all of us lining up to show our hands, face and ears and washing publicly if we were dirty. If anyone was dirty, he or she pumped water into a tin basin that sat on a table at the head of the class and soaped up. So many unidentified things were floating in the well water that we drank and washed in that our teacher pulled the lid off the well one day and instructed Hannon, one of the Nicklie boys to climb down into the well and send up a bucket of water. Thirteen dead mice floated to the surface in the first bucket of water Hannon sent up. That ended our drinking the well water. We still washed in it though.

Freda, my fourth grade teacher, was a large, heavy-bottomed woman with short-cropped hair (which she never combed), a booming voice, dominant personality and mean spirit. She picked on all of us. At recess time, she put us out to play in the coldest weather. In Cantwell, the winter temperatures can fall to -40 for several months. She left us outside and walked to visit Mom. After about an hour one of the kids went to our house to tell her we were freezing and wanted to go back into the schoolhouse. Mom told me that Freda answered the door and when the little boy gave his message, she yelled at him "Get back to school. I'll get there when I'm ready!" After booting the door shut in his face, she stayed longer. Mom didn't really like this teacher and when she heard that we were left outside in the freezing weather, she was outraged but afraid to say anything. That wasn't the extent of Freda's meanness.

Dad made me take cod liver oil every morning as part of his new health regime and one day when I needed help with my math, the teacher smelled the cod liver oil and said in a loud voice, "My God, you stink! Go wash your hands." I pumped water and washed in front of the other kids and I wanted to die. At first, the kids laughed, but when they saw the tears welling up in my eyes from embarrassment, they felt sorry for me and the room went dead quiet. They squirmed in their seats and kept their eyes down knowing how they would feel if it happened to them. I was so upset; I cried all the way home after school. Dad didn't make me take cod liver oil after that.

On her lunch break, Freda tanned a moose hide that she stretched on a piece of plywood set up on sawhorses. She used an Eskimo ulu, (a rounded blade, like a half disc, embedded in a wooden handle). The ulu rocks in a rocking horse fashion for cutting up meat. In tanning, a person scrapes it across the inside of the hide. Freda used her own urine on the hide to keep it wet and loosen the debris on the skin. Tanners used brains or urine to tan hides. I think the acidic nature of the urine also broke down the membranes to make it soft. She smelled from tanning the hide but I don't think she ever noticed.

During that winter, she decided that I should not be left-handed, and insisted that I write with my right hand. I developed a nervous tick of jerking my forearm straight up when I wrote. She finally decided I could go back to my left hand but then she made me turn my hand around instead of upside down, as I had been writing. After that, my handwriting was terrible.

Mom, sick of this teacher's behavior, went to another woman in Cantwell and complained about this teacher being out of control and a bully. With no one to lodge a complaint with in the days of Territorial schools, Mom and the woman decided to do something on their own. When the teacher was in the schoolhouse, Mom and this woman went to the teacher's trailer and put Grandpa's stockpiled Limburger cheese in her stove. Mom said that wasn't her proudest moment, but they couldn't think of any other way to cause her grief. Christmas came and we had some relief from our teacher.

This was the first Christmas we had together with Dad, me, Butch (Dave), and Charlie (John) and Mom who is taking the picture.

Butch and Charlie, my new brother, were both with us for Christmas that year. Butch lived in Palmer with our birth father and Charlie lived in Anchorage with his mom. I loved opening presents that Christmas with a larger family. Mom ordered everything from the Sears and Roebuck or Montgomery Wards catalogs. I was overjoyed with my hard plastic, red nurse's box. The box had a stethoscope, plastic thermometer, plastic hypodermic needle that retracted, and a container of red candy pills in it. The pills were gone by the end of the day and everyone was sick of me taking their temperature and checking their hearts.

I loved tradition and wanted our new family to start our own traditions so Mom made chocolate chiffon pies for Christmas dinner. She also made a fruit salad with canned fruit cocktail, some apples, dates and Dream Whip. As we grew up, we made presents for each other. My aunt told me stories of their Christmas eves past as children in Anchorage. My grandparents invited all of their friends over with their children and all of their gifts. Presents teetered on top of one another stacked high around the tree. Everyone ate and the adults partied while the kids played until the stroke of midnight. At that bewitching hour, Grandpa handed out all of the presents. Because so many people were without extended families in Alaska, people made extended families with their friends and my grandparents had many. Socializing over the long winter months kept cabin fever at bay.

There wasn't much to look forward to as winter dragged on. The Pentecostal Church sent some people to Cantwell to have a church service at their old, log Pentecostal Church. When something new came along, people wanted to go to break the monotony. The church also had a two-story building they built years earlier.

They used part of the two- story building as a school for the local Native kids. When the Natives settled in Cantwell, they worked on the new railroad. Some of the original Natives in the community remembered going to that school. They shared with me that teachers punished them for speaking a word of their own language. It was hard for them to put aside the language with which they had grown up.

This time when the church people came, I talked Dad into taking me. Halfway through the service they gave the call for people to walk the aisle and 'be saved.' I slipped out from beside Dad without his seeing me and up I went to the front of the church. A woman pulled me to my knees and told me to beg God for forgiveness. I didn't know what I had done, but I complied. The guitar player strummed the guitar more forcefully and people on the stage prayed louder and louder until it sounded like wailing. More people came to the front and knelt down for forgiveness. When things quieted down and arms released from around us, we returned to our seats. As we departed from the church, I triumphantly stated, "Dad, I was saved." Dad didn't look at me but exclaimed disgustedly, "Saved from what, A BEAR?" I don't remember the people from the church ever coming back to Cantwell, but then I seriously doubt that Dad would have told me or taken me again.

The river rose in the spring. Water flooded the area right up to our lean-to door. Every bit of the ground from our door to the river flooded. Dad put on hip waders and carried me to school on his back. Then the water froze again and I skated right out the door. When it thawed again, we dug trenches away from the house so it wouldn't run into the lean-to. When the thaw came completely, bridges and roads washed out on every road. We drove over one river on planks and I feared that the car would fall off. Every spring, the rivers swelled from all of the melting snow and ate the banks out on the roads. In a rainy summer, the same thing happened and road crews scrambled to fix washed out roads and bridges.

Dad bought a goat in early spring and we named her Nanny. We let her run lose in the yard and one day while Dad was at work, Mom and I heard Nanny bleating nonstop. Mom ran out the door and saw a large dog attacking and ripping the goat's ear. The goat ran in circles as she tried to get away from the dog who had hold of her ear. Blood flew everywhere. Mom ran into the trailer, grabbed Dad's bolt- action 22- rifle and running out the door, shot the dog. She only wounded it and when she tried to shoot again, a bullet jammed in the barrel. She yelled, "Go get your dad!" I ran down the path to the Road Commission yard as fast as I could but by the time I returned with him, the dog had disappeared. Dad rounded up some friends and all of them searched the woods. Darkness came with snow. Mom and Dad followed the blood trail and wound up at the non-denominational church. It turned out that the dog belonged to the local missionary, Pauline Smith. Mom felt horrible that she had shot the dog and even worse that she had wounded him. The dog made it more than a mile back to Pauline's house but within an hour died from loss of blood.

Pauline came to Cantwell in 1950, by herself. At first, she rented a cabin from Jack West, and then when she acquired a piece of property, she had a house built. After that, she had a church built with her own money. Mom felt terrible when she saw whom the dog belonged to because he was Pauline's only companion. When Mom told her what the dog did to our goat, Pauline understood but the pain on her face showed how much she would miss her companion.

Nanny and me at the lake where we ended up homesteading in 1955.

Nanny grew meaner with age. She ate garbage out of the garbage can, and partially broke off one of her horns ramming into things, like the garbage can. One day, she chased me up on the car and trapped me there for an hour before Mom and Dad came home. I knew if I left the hood of the car, she would nail me. Mom told Dad that Nanny was teaching me bad habits because I copied her by chewing my food with my jaw moving in a circular motion like Nanny did when she chewed her cud. It really irritated Mom but I wasn't even aware that I did it. Nanny and I had baaing contests outside while I hid behind things so she wouldn't get me. She went, "Baa!" and I answered back. We went on like that until something or someone distracted us. One of my distractions came when neighbor kids came by to play.

I played with the Nicklie kids who lived nearby that summer. The Road Commission had a yard of old equipment across the road from their buildings. We loved playing hide 'n seek in old refrigerators and trucks in that yard. It's a scary thought to think of what might have happened if we had not been able to get out of a refrigerator, but back then, we didn't think of dangers like that. We climbed into old trucks, pretended to drive them, and explored every piece of equipment. The practice in those days was to dump old equipment on the flooding riverbanks to keep the water from eating the banks away. All of the equipment we played on was marked for using in that fashion.

Fearing that we would be flooded out again, Dad moved our trailer and lean-to across the road. He picked a spot down the same driveway as my grandparent's house but tucked farther back in the trees. We didn't need to worry about flooding on that side of the road. He made a path through the woods to the Road Commission warehouse where he worked and built a little porch on the lean-to that summer in preparation for winter.

My brother Butch came to stay with us that summer and we had fun building a tree house behind our trailer. He took it over so I retrieved a huge cardboard box from the Road Commission and used it for my own clubhouse. We had a lot of fun outdoors that summer, but sometimes we were too rowdy indoors. One day Dad grabbed both of us by our collars and shoved us outside in the pouring rain with no coats. We were scuffling and passing gas on each other. When Butch sat on my head and passed gas on my face that was enough for Dad. "Out! Both of you. Out!" he yelled as he pushed us out the door.

Every fall, the five Nicklie kids picked a fifty-five gallon barrel of

Our trailer and lean-to with the
hard side tent that our cousins
and Butch and I stayed in for the
summer.

---

blueberries to last their family for the winter. They left the barrel on
their porch and just dipped a cup in the barrel when they wanted blueberries. I only had to pick enough berries for Mom to make jam. The
Cantwell people used to pick blueberries on a hillside close to Jack
River but trees grew on the hillside over the years and soon the berries
on Reindeer Mountain were more plentiful. All of us kids trudged up
the base of Reindeer Mountain and picked for hours. Berries were so
thick we found a patch, knelt down on our knees to pick for a long
time, and then moved on to find another patch. When we picked we
ate some and sometimes we left our buckets nestled in the tundra so we
could roll down the hill on the soft bed of moss and blueberry bushes.
After several hours of picking, we threaded our way down the slope,
through the thicket at the bottom, and onto the gravel road being care-
ful not to spill the results of our labor. Once on the flat of the road, we
raced home in our blueberry stained pants to show our bounty. I never
realized, until it became my job to clean them, that the picking was
easy by comparison.

I rode my bike around our gravel driveway and down the road every
day in the summer. That fall, I hit a big rock and sailed over the han-
dlebars grinding gravel into both knees. Dad swabbed my knees with
hydrogen peroxide as I cried for him to stop. He couldn't get all of the
gravel out of the cuts because I kept shoving his hand away and crying,

"Don't. It hurts too much."

Dad replied, "But there's still gravel in your knees."

"NO! NO! I don't care." I cried.

My knees scarred over with big, dark purple spots under the surface of the skin. When I wore short skirts in high school, kids said, "Alicia, you have something on your knees." I turned red with embarrassment every time someone said it.

Dad took me with him to pick high bush cranberries near the Nenana River in August and we pulled ourselves across the river on the cable cart. We drove out the road east of Cantwell to look for firewood and drove to the dump for discarded building material. Mom didn't like going on these outings because our absence gave her a chance to have some alone time to read.

CHAPTER 3

1956

fall to fall

OUR OLD QUONSET HUT SCHOOL BECAME OUR COMMUNITY THEATRE that year. Long, hard, wooden benches were lined up for us to sit on. They ordered Kohl's popcorn to sell and the whole community turned out for the "Ma and Pa Kettle" films. People stomped the packed snow off their boots and shed their heavy coats as they settled in to socialize before the movie started. It was the only place to socialize in the community aside from the church. A buzz of conversation from adults and kids filled the Quonset. If the filmstrip broke, as it often did, we resumed our babble until they spliced it and the show went on. Sometime after that, they showed movies at the FAA station in Summit, instead of in Cantwell. That was fine when the roads were decent, but sometimes the roads were bad with ice or a whiteout and I sat home moping all evening.

Bea, a woman who lived about a mile from us, offered to teach me to knit. I walked to her house on Saturdays and spent about an hour or two knitting. One day a terrible storm came up while I was at her house. It snowed and gusting winds whipped the snow into a total whiteout with a temperature of minus thirty degrees. That didn't even factor in the wind chill. We were used to the minus temperatures so I thought nothing of the dropping temperature when I went to her house. With the weather turning bad so quickly, Bea said, "Maybe it would be best if you went home before the weather gets worse." Since there were no phones from house to house, Bea couldn't call and see if I made it home. I waded through the snow unable to see anything, totally disoriented. I groped my way along, slower and slower, straining to see through the blowing snow. Soon I chilled to the bone, sleepiness overcame me, and I lay down beside the road and went to sleep. A family friend driving by in his pickup saw a snow covered lump beside the road and stopped to investigate. Within one block of our house, I fell asleep and lay freezing to death. The man lifted me out of the snow and drove me home where I went through hell for the next few hours as they put my feet and hands in lukewarm water and put warm wraps on my ears. I frostbit my hands, feet and ears and when those parts thawed, I cried from the "pins and needles" pain.

Bill and Jennie Nancarrow, a young, childless couple who occasionally needed a kid- fix invited me to spend the next weekend with them. They lived about seventeen miles north of Cantwell on the way to McKinley Park. I ate too much at dinner and threw up later that night. I think that about cured their kid-fix. Bill took me out with him to feed his sled dogs and let me watch as he cooked up a cauldron of cornmeal and salmon. I slopped the mess into the eight dog dishes and handed them out as the dogs jumped up and down on their doghouses yipping and barking. I felt so important. It wasn't much fun helping at home, but when it was work somewhere else, it took on new meaning. In the evening, Bill showed me the beautiful dog sleds he made. He even made miniature ones. Sometimes, when they had me over in the future, I just sat and listened as they visited with their friends, Valentine (who had a reputation for making coffee a person could cut with a knife) and Charlie Ott, a well-known photographer. Before bedtime, I sat watching as Jenny combed out her long hair, which streamed down her back. In the morning, she put it all into a bun and no one except for Bill and I ever knew how long it was. After combing her hair, Jenny climbed up the log ladder to their loft and quiet prevailed. Bill built her a beautiful house on the other side of the lake from where their cabin sat but she died of cancer before they moved in. They were so nice to me that I stored them in my heart as special people in my life.

Someone gave Dad some grizzly bear meat, which he cooked for dinner one night. Unsure of how to cook it, he put it in the oven as a roast. After a few hours the whole house smelled so bad, we gagged and ran out the door. I can't even describe the smell other than to say, "Horrible." We found out later that black bear is good, but not grizzly bear. We evacuated to Grandma and Grandpa's house for the day to let the house air out. Dad never cooked grizzly bear meat again. We were always eating different things when Dad cooked. If he brought squirrel home, he and I ate it. Mom wouldn't touch it. He picked things from nature and tried them in wild concoctions. One winter after my brother came to live with us, Dad went through a soy period. One night he made make-believe clams from soy when Butch was with us. They were so bad that neither Butch nor I could get them down. I tried to swallow but they wouldn't go down. Butch whispered to me, "Move them as far back in your cheek as you can pack them." When we left the table, we immediately went into the bathroom and spit them into the toilet.

I couldn't believe that Mom would make us eat all those weird things because she told me about a babysitter she had who insisted that she and my aunt drink her refrigerated breast milk. Mom said she gagged on the milk but the babysitter made her drink it anyway. This same babysitter made her eat the fat on meat because she knew Mom hated it. We expected Mom to be more compassionate on this issue but she wouldn't intervene. Dad joined an "Around the World" food club and we had another whole season of eating fried ants, chocolate covered bumblebees, snails, and squid to mention a few. Dad was an adventurous eater. Sometimes it got him into trouble like the night he writhed in pain with ptomaine poisoning from some concoction he made. He threw up, groaned and banged his head against the wall beside the bed all night. He never cooked anything the way the recipe read. He added whatever to try something new. I have to say though that he made the best bread I have ever eaten. There were so many things in it that it was a meal in itself. Eating was interesting in our home but getting out to see things was more interesting to me.

Maggie, one of my friends, came to visit one day and invited me to walk two miles down to the Native village to visit Grandma Anne Nicklie, an Athabaskan Native. We lifted the tarp covering her front

A cow moose with her calves in the misty morning.

door (the tarp cut down the cold air coming in during the winter) and entered the semi-dark cabin. There was a pungent odor of wood smoke, and cooked meat. As we sat on the floor in front of Grandma Anne, Maggie translated from Athabaskan to English. This woman was old with a very lined face and milky eyes. She gently reached out her bony hand and put it on mine as she talked. I sat mesmerized and a little impatient when Maggie talked to her and didn't translate for me. The woman showed me some of her needlework, but I didn't know what she said. We had tea and then left. Even at the age of ten, I realized how special that day was in meeting this very wise Athabaskan grandmother in the village. I wish I could have had a real conversation with her.

Maggie came often to take me on outings. I knew we would have an adventure and I looked forward to it. One day, she came to get me for a jaunt downtown. We passed a coffin-like wooden box on the edge of the bank next to the road. The box measured about two and a half feet tall, with a pitched roof like a house. I asked her what it was and she told me it was a Spirit House where a Native boy was buried. It is the Athabaskan Native custom to build a Spirit House over the top of the grave and place the dead person's favorite possessions in the house or at the head of it. We went to the grave to take a closer look at the clock and cup at the head of this boy's house. His mother came out of her cabin a short distance up the road and pointed a rifle at us. Maggie talked to her in Athabaskan and told her we weren't there to hurt the grave site. Fanny Secondchief, the boy's mother, grew more agitated and she kept yelling at us in Athabaskan until we moved away from the grave. As we passed by her cabin, we saw her watching us from her small cabin window. Maggie told me that the boy fell out of a tree and had internal injuries but fearing his mother would be angry with the boys he played with, he kept quiet and lay in pain. Maggie went on to tell me about how brave Fanny was. She encountered a bear in the middle of the stream she crossed and with her baby on her back, she killed the bear with a hatchet. Fannie only had one son still living and he lived with her.

Butch came to live with us full time that summer. He made friends with a boy named Robert, and they hung out together exploring trails and climbing nearby mountains but as fall approached, they got more than they bargained for. A big cow moose with calves chased them up a tree one day. Butch climbed one tree and Robert followed up the same tree. Butch yelled, "It won't hold us both. Find your own tree!" Robert made it down the tree and up another and there the two stayed. Our teacher drove by on the road and Butch and Robert yelled and waved but the teacher just thought they were being sociable and waved back. They continued to yell as the car drove out of sight but no brake lights came on. Every time the cow moose left the area under the trees, the boys tried to climb down but she came charging back and up the tree they went again. The afternoon passed slowly until they thought they would never be able to escape. Eventually she moved on with her babies to forage elsewhere and they backed down their respective trees and raced home.

Things were never dull. Butch and I were clowning around one day and I crossed my eyes. People say it's not true that a person's eyes can lock, but mine did. They locked and I jerked them back. It pulled a muscle in my eye and I wore a patch over my eye for a month. I looked like a pirate. When I say that things were never dull, I think of our trips to Kantishna on the harrowing road around narrow corners.

Dad liked to visit a man named Johnny Busia who lived at Kantishna. Kantishna was at one time a gold mining community called Eureka. To reach this place we traveled ninety long miles on a winding, gravel road into McKinley Park. That meant we had to go around Polychrome Pass, a pass with steep grades and winding curves on a road too narrow for two cars to pass and a drop off edge that terrified me. There were no guardrails to keep a car from going over the edge so we hugged the inside of the road next to the bluffs, but on the return home, we were literally on the edge overlooking a steep ravine. I sat next to the door when Mom went along and that's when Dad joked, "Boy, these brakes just aren't working very well. They must have gotten wet." It wasn't funny to me as I looked over the edge around every corner. To add to my fear, Dad drove too fast and always looked elsewhere. If he saw flowers in the ditch, he said, "Look at those flowers over there" and headed right for the ditch. Every time we went, I had nightmares that night about us sailing off the cliff into midair for a long drop to the bottom.

Mr. Busia's cabin sat on the high bank on the other side of Moose River. Once we arrived, we pulled ourselves across the river via an Alaska tram. An anchored cable stretched across the river with a pulley wheel attached to the cable and a short, board platform swung below the pulley. Dad did a hand-over-hand to pull us across the river. I straddled the board and held my feet up on the board to keep the water from soaking me. It was a scary crossing as I dangled above the raging river on this board swaying back and forth. We couldn't all go at the same time, so Dad pulled Mom across and then came back for me.

Johnny Busia was a small 5'4" man. He talked so fast, I couldn't understand him. He came from Croatia and joined his father at Kantishna in 1918. His father had mined and trapped there since the early 1900s and after he died, Johnny stayed on. His log cabin sat right on the edge of the bank overlooking Moose River. During the gold stampede, there was a community of 2000 miners there when the place was called Eureka. All but a few had moved away. Johnny had an old, arthritic, Malamute Husky that lay chained to his doghouse. I bent over to pet his thick, matted fur, but he didn't show any enthusiasm. His eyes were cloudy with age and his arthritic body moved slowly. The heavy chain anchored to his collar seemed too much for him as he lay there with his big head on his paws and his eyes closed. He barely opened them when I walked up to him.

Inside Johnny's dim lit one-room cabin were two board bunks, a cooking stove and a table with two chairs. I always sat on one of the beds. If Mom came, Johnny invited her to sit at the table and he grabbed a log to sit on. Within minutes of our entering the cabin, Johnny climbed down through a trap door in his floor and brought up some of his home brew made of molasses, rice, hops, and sugar. When he pulled the cork off, it popped with a loud pop like champagne. Mom always declined, so he and Dad sat and polished off the bottle and as the liquor disappeared, Johnny talked faster and Dad laughed louder, slapping his knee with every funny story. Johnny always brought up an apple for me, but after he spit on it and polished it on his faded, flannel shirt, I didn't really want to eat it. I politely said, "thank you" and then quietly left the cabin to try to feed it to his dog. Since the dog never showed any interest, it left me no alternative but to eat it. After my brother came to live with us, Mom stopped going on these excursions and Butch and I went with Dad. Butch, being more creative than I, threw his apple in the river after Johnny spit on it and I followed suit. On the rides home from Johnny's, Dad edged even closer to the cliff's edge and I held my breath and closed my eyes. At some point, we stopped going for our visits and I heard that Johnny Busia died in his sleep. They shot and buried his old dog with him.

Dad decided he wanted to homestead acreage on what we then called Four Mile Lake so he filled out all of the paperwork with the State for a one hundred and twenty acre homestead and excavated a spot to build an earth house. Congress passed The Homestead Act of 1862 enabling anyone more than twenty-one to homestead up to one hundred sixty acres for twenty dollars. The homesteader had to meet a living requirement on the land as well as the requirements of building a house and farming ten percent of the property within five years. In 1976, the act was repealed in other states but Alaska had an extension until 1986.

With payments, Dad acquired a big 6x6 Army truck with a winch and after enlisting help from the railroad extra-gang crew, on the

This truck is very similar to our 6x6 but ours had a winch.

---

weekends, they set about digging out a hole in the lake bank for an earth house. This crew of six young, very fit men and Dad shoveled sand into the big bucket attached to the winch and then moved the bucket to a dumping area. These men had nothing to do on weekends and loved the idea of helping someone build something from scratch. Fortunately for Dad his friend Jonsie, the railroad station manager, was his way in with the extra-gang crew. Dad told them that Mom would cook them home cooked meals on the weekends and they were all for that. Digging out a hole big enough for a proposed bedroom, living room, and kitchen went slowly, but they kept at it every weekend. It was a laborious task to maneuver the big metal bucket filled with sand.

Dad built a raft during this same period and anchored it to the shore for Mom to cook on. The raft, equipped with a wood cook stove and a cot enabled Dad to sleep there if they worked too late. I asked Mom why Dad built a raft for the cooking instead of just cooking on shore. She said, "I don't know. You know everything your father does is a bit different." After eating the evening meal, the extra gang crew sat around talking and laughing. Dad loved to bounce his ideas off people and glean their input. He tried new things all the time and appeared to be ahead of his time.

He and the crew dug out the whole kitchen area, put the spruce logs up for the walls and ceiling and then buried the top with sand again. The living room and bedroom areas had their back walls into the bank with the front side out of the bank facing the lake. Life at the lake only took place on weekends and the rest of the time, we had lives in Cantwell.

Dad sent our Nanny goat for breeding and she had babies that summer. We named them Oney and Twoy and they were into everything just like Nanny had been when she was a kid. We loaded all three goats into the back of our 4x4, a smaller Army truck than the 6x6, and took them with us to meet the train and pick up the daily mail. Picking up the mail gave us a chance to visit with the local people and wave at the train passengers. The train whistle blew and then came barreling around the bend into the small settlement of downtown Cantwell. As the train screeched to a stop, passengers crowded the openings between the railroad cars to take pictures of our goats as they jumped up on the cab of the truck and leaned out from the open sides of the truck to stare at the passengers. That must have been some sight from the passenger's standpoint–three goats and two grinning kids posed for a picture.

The goats were fun but work as well. Butch and I were expected to keep their stalls clean in the little goat shed and to milk Nanny. We took turns with the milking but when Butch's turn came, he squirted

The train was our lifeline in those days.

me every time I came around the corner. Several times, I dripped with milk and there wasn't much in the bucket to take indoors. Sometimes Nanny held her milk and we had to go back later in the evening to milk her again. That's the excuse my brother used when there wasn't much milk left after one of his 'let's drench the sister' episodes. Dad strained, heated and refrigerated the milk and I loved it. When we didn't have the goat's milk, we drank powdered or canned Carnation evaporated milk, which I didn't care for.

Butch and I constantly looked for things to do. An old abandoned cabin sat off the road in the trees and Butch decided to make it a haunted house to scare two Cantwell boys called the Hocking boys. Their dad worked as a grader operator on the road. The boys were so innocent that they believed everything Butch told them. He found a table knife, tin plates, and an old bottle of catsup in the cupboards of the old cabin and set about making his haunted house. First, he stabbed a knife into the front door with catsup dripping down, and then put the tin plates on the table, dripped catsup across the floor, and last of all he tipped the chairs over. Then he went home to put on hip waders for the flooded basement and to get matches. He told me to bring the boys back by telling them that I had something grand to show them. I ran to their cabin and excitedly exclaimed, "Come quick. I have something to

My brother Butch (Dave) and I clowning around.

---

show you!" They asked, "What? But I wouldn't tell. When we arrived at the cabin, smoke curled from a corner of the cabin where Butch lit some moss to smolder. When we entered the cabin, Butch moaned. He moaned, groaned and whimpered as he sloshed back and forth in the basement water. One of the brothers wet his pants and then they shot out the door and down the overgrown driveway so fast, I hardly had a chance to see their exit. Butch loved playing tricks and one day when they came to our house to play, he told them they had to get down on their knees and bow to the floor in front of Mom's statues of Amman Hotep and Nefertiti sitting on the shelf. Butch cracked up when they did it. He made me laugh all the time even if it was a joke on me. Butch became more serious that summer though.

Our birth father passed away of a massive heart attack at the age of thirty-eight that summer. Butch had spent more time with him and felt guilty for having come to live with us. Dad wanted to adopt us after our birth father passed away so in the fall we all went to Anchorage where we appeared before a judge and finalized the paperwork. We were a family. Things seemed to be going very well since Dad had won the bid on the school bus contract to supplement our income. Then school started.

CHAPTER 4

1957

fall to fall

Our new school when I was in the fifth grade. It had two classrooms and the teacher's quarters.

CONTRACTORS BUILT A NEW TWO- ROOM SCHOOL WITH ATTACHED teacher's quarters that summer and we moved in to our new school.

As soon as we headed out on our walk to school, Butch pulled out his cigarettes. He started smoking when he came to Cantwell and he wasn't willing to give it up. Once out of the house, he puffed away. As we walked to school, he bet me he could stop smoking. First he said, "I'll bet you my Brownie camera I can quit smoking," as he threw his pack of cigarettes into the bar ditch. But, by the end of the day, he frantically searched in the grass for his pack. He drew me in again, "I'll bet you my bongo drums I can quit smoking" but I won those as well. He just couldn't give up cigarettes. Even after Dad caught him and punished him, he never gave them up.

For Halloween, Butch and Robert put someone's outhouse on barrels in the middle of the road going down to the store. They snickered about it all the next morning but they wouldn't tell me whose outhouse they stole. I wondered what the people thought in the morning when they made their mad dash to the outhouse only to find a hole and no house.

The days became shorter with daylight showing up from 10 AM to 2 PM. We walked to and from school with a flashlight, in the dark.

That winter, I rode the bus route to Summit with Dad every time there was a white out. Wind swirled falling snow until everything on and around the road blurred into solid white. That made it impossible to see anything, much less the road. I walked in front of the VW bus so Dad could follow me and stay on the road. The wind blew piercingly cold and I squinted to keep the snow out of my eyes. Sometimes my eyes burned from the glare of the snow but I had to do it to make the bus route. I rode in the bus for a ways and then got out for a bad stretch. I looked at these outings as respite from my brother since he was always thumping on me.

Butch picked on me whenever Mom and Dad went somewhere. He started by initiating a pillow fight that always escalated until I ended in tears. One evening, he kicked me with his big heavy winter boots on and left a big bruise on my shin. Afraid to tell Mom and Dad about it, I dreamed of revenge. The bruise on the leg solidified it. Fed up, I sent for a Charles Atlas kit to build up my muscles. The ad showed the before-- scrawny man picture and then the after-- muscle built-up man. I wanted to beat my brother up for a change. When the kit came, so did a bill for some outrageous sum. I wrote a tearful letter:

Dear Charles Atlas,
I am not a man. I am only a girl who wanted to be strong
so I could beat up on my brother for a change. I saw on the
magazine page that it said "Absolutely Free." I will give this
back unharmed because it said free.

Upset that I might have to pay for it, I fretted for a week. I thought Mom mailed my letter, but she thought it was so funny she kept it and sent the kit back. A day came shortly after that letter when my brother hit his friend Robert, after Robert hit me on the playground. He gave Robert a nosebleed. Butch never picked on me after that. From that point on, he became my protector.

Robert pinched the girls on their nipples and disrupted the class. One day, as one of the girls put on her coat to make a dash for the outhouse, he barred the girl's way in the coatroom and she threw up all over him. No one felt sorry for him.

Even with no phones in Cantwell, news travelled fast. The night Robert's house caught on fire, people came from every direction to help. With no fire department, the effort proved futile. People ended up standing around to watch as flames consumed the house. I felt sorry for Robert even though he had been mean to all the girls. I couldn't imagine losing everything.

In the evenings after school, Butch and I stayed inside to read or do homework. After we went to bed at night, Mom baked and polished floors when everyone was out of the way. We heard the polisher going and smelled the delicious smell of chocolate cake as the aroma drifted down the hall and sometimes it was hard to stay in bed knowing there was a chocolate cake sitting on the kitchen counter.

Some nights, Butch played freeze-out with me. He slept on the top bunk and kept his window wide open. I burrowed down under my covers on the lower bunk and took it as long as I could but if I couldn't breath and had to put my head above the covers, I saw my breath. I whined, "I'm freezing. Butch, close the window!" Sometimes Mom opened our door because she could feel the cold draft coming from under the door. She would say, "Close that window! It's freezing in here" and that ended Butch tormenting me.

Early winter dragged by with no visitors so the day a big, burly man with a bushy beard, unruly hair and one partially- closed eye came to see Dad, Butch and I were all ears around the corner. The man looked like a pirate and I felt uneasy.

Dad went to college in Spearfish, South Dakota, and then took two years of law school from the Blackstone School of Law when he first arrived in Cantwell and people, knowing that he studied law, came to him with legal questions.

Dad took the man into another room to talk about the man's problem and Butch and I whispered back and forth that the man looked like a killer. Dad discussed it later with Mom and we overheard that the man asked, "If someone killed someone in self defense, would they go to prison?" We didn't catch the rest of the details but Butch assured me that the question wasn't hypothetical. The man never came back, much to my relief.

In December, my gums swelled and my teeth were all loose so Mom took me on the train to a doctor in Anchorage. I had Pyorrhea, an inflammation of the teeth sockets. The doctor told Mom I couldn't have anything solid or my teeth would fall out. I saw television for the first time at my grandparents' house on that trip. When we returned to Cantwell, I lay around in misery for three weeks drinking only fluids through a straw. Christmas fell during that time and Mom and Dad gave me a large box of chocolates from the Montgomery Wards catalog. Kids came to see me as I mended and each time they spied the big box of chocolates, they asked if they could have one or two pieces. Then Mom, Dad and Butch helped themselves and before I knew it, the box was empty. I didn't get one piece of the candy before I healed. Kids never forget things like that.

Mr. Van Wingerden, the new missionary replacing Pauline Smith, came that winter with a trove of exciting things in store to entice us to Young People's Meetings on Friday nights. We skied on Reindeer Mountain after he took the time to drag a light plant (generator for light) up the steep hill. I received a pair of skis from Mom and Dad for Christmas and on my first trip down the hill, I flipped a somersault and broke both of them. We played hockey and ice-skated on the lake where we built our homestead the next summer. Mr. Van Wingerden pulled us on a toboggan tied to the back of his van. We screamed with delight and a bit of fear as we shot around the corners of the road and careened off the snow piled embankments. There were about six of us on the toboggan clutching on to each other for dear life. One time, we shot off the side of the bridge, when we were too far to the right. The rope caught on the corner of the bridge and the toboggan snapped back dumping the others over the side. Somehow, my coat caught on the toboggan and by the time I tore loose, the whole front of my red snow coat ripped from top to bottom. I had a nosebleed and lost my gloves. After the initial scare, we were ready to go again the following week.

At the end of our outdoor time, we went the preacher's home, had popcorn, Kool-Aid, and a Bible lesson. There were times when we stayed inside and played games because of the weather. On one occasion we played "Meet the Fly Family" One of the kids stayed in another room while we were told our parts. This kid, led in by another person, went down the row of "the fly family" as we each introduced ourselves. The unsuspecting kid moved down the row to meet Mrs. Horsefly, then Mr. Housefly, Miss Butterfly, Master Shoofly and then Baby Let-Her-Fly who swatted the kid with a wet sponge in the face. That brought howls of laughter from everyone.

This nondenominational church was not the only religious entity in Cantwell though. In fact, they didn't have as much of a toehold in Cantwell as the Russian Orthodox Church had earlier. Russian priests made annual trips to small Ahtna (Athabaskan) villages like Cantwell as late as the 1950s. Maggie said they wore black robes and went from cabin to cabin swinging their incense burners. Some of the orthodox traditions are still in the villages, like the double cross with the crooked lower bar and the fences around the graves. The Natives still kept their own traditions as well with the houses over the graves and the favorite possessions put at the gravesite.

I had Young People's meetings to look forward to as my constant but Dad varied the things he did in his spare time. He tried taxidermy on a few owls but decided he liked to paint pictures more than stuff birds. He painted a haunting picture of a woman in a ground length, hooded coat standing at the edge of a cliff with an old dead tree in the foreground. The colors in the picture were dead, dark colors and the whole picture gave me a sense of hopelessness. I wondered if she wanted to jump and I used to stand and stare at the picture. I read emotions into it. I imagined that she felt loneliness and depression and was too far out on the ledge for anyone to save her. The image of that picture never left me.

Then he started painting Alaska scenery of snowy mountains, trees, and old cabins. That's when he sold his artwork.

February came with Valentine's Day and Dad bought a box of 24 mint patties. He unwrapped each one, wrote a love note to enclose, and then rewrapped each mint for Mom. I thought it was the sweetest thing I had ever seen. Since I didn't have any money, I usually wrote Mom or Dad a little note telling them that for their birthday or Christmas I would give them so many days of labor. For Mom it was, "I will clean house for you for one week." For Dad I wrote, "I will do whatever chore you don't want to do for one week." Sometimes, I made gifts but they usually found their way to the garbage because they weren't that nice.

Dad hard at work painting.

Dad always came up with different things to do in the winter. One day he decided to hypnotize me and Mom said, "Everett, are you sure you know what you're doing? What if she doesn't come out of it?" He hypnotized me even though Mom argued with him about it and when I was hypnotized, he hung on my arm to show Mom how rigid I could be under hypnosis. I don't know whether he tired of it or Mom forbade him to do it because he never did it again. It seemed that he tried anything to stave off cabin fever.

For a small community, Cantwell had things going on all the time. There were bingo games at the school and our school threw a Valentine's Dance on February 9 for grades 4, 5, 6, 7, and 8. A big snowstorm hit and the Summit people couldn't come because of drifting snow. The Cantwell people at the dance had to eat all of the ice cream and cake—much to our delight. We even had music with two local men, Wilson Nickolai and Roy Tansy, playing guitars.

Our school put out the *Windy Press* paper and in March, it read like this:

A Mister Rabbit at Summit eats at Hall's Deluxe Porch
Restaurant. Several dogs have invited him for dinner,
but so far, he has declined the offer.

The paper went on to say that my dad, Mr. Skipper and Mr. Bowman showed up at school with a snowplow, pickup and black sedan to take kids back to Summit because high winds and blowing snow made the roads dangerous. They took the kids as far as the railroad tracks near Summit and someone came to pick them up from there. On the way back to Cantwell, Mr. Skipper flipped the snowplow over. He wasn't hurt. The paper even had ads in it like: "Black puppy needs good home, Guaranteed to pull sled in one year." The next paper, put out in May, was loaded with facts. Who had surgery, who won the Summit Ice Pool for the ice breaking up on Summit Lake, and what students were going to do in the summer were interesting bits of information. Readers of the paper learned that the Nicklie and Tansy families moved into their new houses out of the village that year. One boy announced he planned to teach his puppies to pull a sled, get some new girlfriends and catch ground squirrels. The May issue made us all anxious for summer.

With nothing else to do except read all the time, I looked for things to do and even went so far as to beg Dad, "Please let me roll your cigarettes for you." He had a little cigarette- rolling contraption. I placed a long cigarette paper in the bottom of the roller, sprinkled tobacco in, tamped it with my finger, and then pulled the rollers over the top of the long cigarette to roll it tight and seal it. I then pushed on the blade to come down and cut the cigarette into three cigarettes of normal size. It's a good thing I never liked cigarettes, because I had easy access to all I wanted. Things slowed down so much that winter that we were all bored. Mom needed respite from the dark winter days and she found her way out.

She left on the train to go into Anchorage and shop. She always stayed with Grandma and Grandpa and while she was there, a little, two foot long, shorthaired, mongrel dog with floppy ears and big eyes squeezed through the fence at my grandparents' home in Mountain View, a suburb of Anchorage, and stood shivering on the porch. The little dog stood there holding up one white paw and then another. Mom felt sorry for her and begged Grandma to let her come in. When Mom left Anchorage, the dog went with her and I then had a little dog with a white stripe down her forehead, around her muzzle and on her paws. I named her Frosty and we were inseparable. For some unknown reason, I stopped calling her Frosty and called her Pedie Rue instead. It struck me as more affectionate than Frosty. Whenever I sat down, she lay in my lap and when she wasn't in my lap, she sat watching me with her big, brown, damp eyes.

When spring finally came to Cantwell, my parents took a picture of me standing on the cab of the car reaching as high as I could to touch the top of the snow berm beside the road. We had our share of snow that winter with twelve feet of snow bermed beside the road.

The long awaited summer came and the dreariness of winter faded. Trees budded out, and the Fireweed with its beautiful fuchsia colored blossoms brightened the landscape. I made soapberry pies with the girls that lived down a back path from our house. Their small, dilapidated cabin sat facing the Denali Highway with a low, sagging roof and only a few small windows. It was a dark cabin so we always stayed outside to play. We borrowed pie tins from our mothers to make our soapberry pies. Soapberries looked very similar to high bush cranberries and newcomers often mistook the two, only to get a stomachache

My little dog Frosty (Pedie Rue).

on the Soapberries. I borrowed Mom's hand mixer and we beat the berries into a high mound of froth and then dumped them into pie tins making believe they were meringue pies. They weren't edible but we felt like little chefs.

My friend Ruby and I climbed to the top of Reindeer Mountain. The base of the mountain sat next to the Denali Highway. Once we reached the top of the mountain, it was so cold that Ruby took the burnable inserts out of her shoes and burned them to warm our hands. It was hard to keep our footing on the unstable shale-covered ground. After hours of climbing just to say we did it, we stood on the top and looked over the whole valley with little dots of cabins sitting here and there. The only creatures up there with us were families of ptarmigan birds strutting over the hillside.

Duffy Tyone, a friend of our family, took me hunting for Indian potatoes along the riverbank a few weeks later. He said, "We used to eat the potatoes all the time but the young people have lost the ways of the older people and don't eat the things from nature anymore." The

Indian potatoes were roots of a certain plant and very hard to find as we realized that day. He also showed me a plant the Natives called Goose. It tasted like rhubarb with little hairs on the outside. There were berries all over for harvesting and he showed them all to me. All of the berries he showed me were edible.

Maggie took me for jaunts down back trails and told me of the olden days in Cantwell. One day we passed a still pond where we spotted a nice fourteen-inch landlocked grayling. Maggie gathered up a bundle of grass and lying down on her belly, slowly slipped her hand in the water along the bank with the bundle of grass hiding her hand. She waited for the fish as he slowly swam past and then she circled around him from the backside with the clump of grass and in an upward sweep of her hand, flipped the unsuspecting fish out of the water onto the bank. He flopped around vigorously and was close to slipping back into the pond but she jumped up and stepped on him. The rest became history since he became her dinner that night. I was in awe of the things she did.

She also took me to falling down corrals with rotting wood. She told me that men used them in the past to herd reindeer in Cantwell. I had heard about the history of the reindeer from Grandpa but never saw the corrals. Grandpa told me that in 1921, a herd of more than 1100 government- owned reindeer was driven from Goodnews Bay on the Bering Sea to Cantwell. It took a year to cross the 1200 miles. Originally, they transplanted the reindeer from Russia to an area close to the Bering Strait between Russia and Alaska. Grandpa said they brought them to Cantwell for the Natives to take care of and sell the meat. The Cantwell area was ideal for the reindeer because of range-lands for winter and summer grazing. The new railroad made it appealing, since the meat and hides could be shipped out on the rail. It wasn't an easy trip with dog sled's going through the ice as well as extreme cold, wolves dragging reindeer down and reindeer that left the herd to join with the caribou herds. Grandpa's story didn't have a happy ending because the reindeer herds were only in existence for six years. The herders didn't stay long, salaries were low, government subsidies halted, and the project fizzled. The reindeer dwindled in numbers because of wolves and the rest joined with the caribou herd that migrated through. I loved the history that Grandpa shared with me and when I grew up, I researched everything I could find on Cantwell. That's when I learned that in 1923 a silent movie was made in Cantwell titled, *Lure of the Yukon* using the reindeer herd. In some of Jack Luick's (the filmmakers) notes about the movie, he wrote that while he was working on one movie in Alaska he went to look at the reindeer herd in Cantwell on a whim. He was so enthusiastic about the reindeer that he wrote a story using the herd and the Cantwell area. The movie was action packed about the gold rush and a villain who blew off the top of a bluff with dynamite in an attempt to bury his wife and the other people below.

Grandpa could tell me the history stories, but on our outings, Maggie walked me through the visual experience. Whenever anyone came along wanting to go anywhere, I bounded out the door to explore.

Two boys, Stony and Munson, went with me one day to explore the brush (that's what we called the heavy undergrowth of bushes) at the base of Reindeer Mountain. As we pushed through the bushes in an area that had always had ice in the past, we stopped dead in our tracks when we saw what appeared to be a big, dead, coiled up snake. There are no snakes in Alaska but we had seen pictures of them and without hesitation, Monson grabbed a stick, moved in and demolished it. He mashed it up like mayonnaise. Stony and I wanted to take a closer look at it but there wasn't anything to look at but a pile of mush. Dad said the snakelike blob was probably a fresh water eel or burbot that made it up some stream and then the stream eventually dried up. It sure looked like a snake the way it coiled. Here we thought we had made some monumental discovery, but it turned out there are a few eels that make it up the steams. Dad caught a burbot in one of the streams later and I can say that our snakelike thing didn't look at all like a burbot.

It wasn't all fun that summer. One nice summer day I sat reading a book when Dad came home for lunch. "Get out of this house and do something outside!" he scolded.

"There isn't anything to do," I answered.

"Grab a fishing pole and go fishing at Fish Creek" he retorted. I did just that but after about two casts out, I caught my hook in the nearby brush that bordered the stream. As I reached back into the bushes to free the hook, I dropped the pole and the fishing line jerked down as I reached back for the line and embedded the fishhook in my thumb.

The Carlson/West Roadhouse and Store when they made the movie in Cantwell called the *Lure of the Yukon* in 1923.

I didn't want to go home empty-handed so I yelled across the stream to my friend, Munson, "Monson, I'll pay you a dollar for the graying you just caught." He declined and wouldn't budge in his decision. I offered him more and told him, "Dad will be mad at me if I go home with a hook in my thumb and nothing to show for it." However, he still wasn't moved. When I returned home, Dad wasn't mad when he saw the fishhook. He just shook his head. They tried pulling the hook out, but it seated itself deeper. That night my thumb throbbed as I tried to sleep and by the next morning, it was swollen and inflamed. Mom drove me to the McKinley Park Hotel, thirty miles away, to see the nurse, but when the nurse sprayed a freezing compound on it and then proceeded to hack at it with a razor blade, the pain was unbearable. I tried hard not to cry, but it came to a point that I could no longer hold back the tears. With the thumb being only partially frozen, I felt every slice of the razor. The nurse, feeling faint, went to the open window for fresh air. She told Mom she just couldn't get the hook and I'd have to go elsewhere. My thumb swelled more and throbbed nonstop. For five days, everyone who came along tried to remove the fishhook and my thumb swelled to twice its normal size. Mom decided to take me in the opposite direction, ten miles away, to Summit. A woman lived there who had some nurse's training. The woman immediately called an Anchorage doctor who told her to put a rubber band on my thumb for a few minutes and then jerk the hook out with the pliers. She did just that and blood gushed all over the place. Anyone seeing it would have thought she cut my thumb off. I healed but never cared much for fishing after that.

The church Young People's Meetings continued throughout the summer. We swam in a nearby lake, played badminton, volleyball and tetherball. On one of these evenings, I watched the kids standing outside Mr. Van Wingerden's house while he was inside making popcorn. The kids had little waxed paper blobs of something, which they were divvying up amongst themselves. It turned out to be Star chewing tobacco that they mixed with ashes from burned cottonwood burls. They stuffed the tobacco into their cheek pockets or into the area below their front teeth and while they were doing this, one of the kids asked if I wanted some, but I declined. Then on another night of the meetings, I accepted when asked again. We were in the back of Mr. Van Wingerden's van on the way to my house to ask if I could go swimming with the kids. As my mouth filled with saliva and this golden colored mush, I asked the kids, "Where can I spit. They answered in unison, "No, no. You can't spit." When my mouth filled to capacity, I swallowed. We arrived at my house and as I jumped out of the van and headed up the little path to our front door, I stumbled on the big rocks bordering the path and fell flat on my face. I couldn't focus and felt light-headed but knew I needed to carry this off so I could go swimming. I concentrated on my feet and made it to the door. Once inside the house, I made a beeline for the bathroom to spit the rest of the tobacco out. I yelled to Mom in the kitchen, "Can I go swimming with all the kids?" When I heard the "Yes," I staggered into the bedroom for my swimsuit and left before she could see me holding onto the walls as I weaved my way back to the front door.

I tried tobacco one more time when Maggie and I were hanging out. She gave me some just before Mom sent me to Grandpa and Grandma's house to get something out of the basement. Fortunately, for me no one was home. I reached the top step of the steep stairs to the basement and that heady feeling hit me. I missed the top step and tumbled all the way to the bottom onto a cement floor. It's a good thing kids are resilient because after lying there for a few minutes, I got up and limped home. I never tried chewing again.

Cantwell kids always found something to do. We had foot races down the gravel road, played baseball in the road until 1 AM with the summer sun up all night. Sometimes we just walked downtown to the store for something to do. One day, Butch, Robert and I walked down to the Cantwell store just to pass time. Once inside the store, I saw Robert and my brother whispering and laughing. All of a sudden, they raced out the door and ran down to the stream nearby on the path to the village. I didn't know what they were up to, but I knew that the way they ran out of the store, it couldn't be good so I ran as well. It took me a bit to catch up with them and there they were opening a jar of pickled pigs feet and sampling them. They offered me some but I declined. I couldn't believe that they would steal from my friend Mr. West. It turned out that they didn't even like the pigs feet and threw the rest into the stream.

I decided I would rather hang out with my friend Ruby, instead of Butch and Robert, because I knew I wouldn't get into any trouble with her. She came to visit me or I visited at her house constantly. I ate at her house so much I think her parents thought they had adopted me. Ruby's mom, Lily, was a fantastic cook and I loved the smell of her stew when I stayed for dinner. They had a huge wood stove in their kitchen and it was always hot. When she made stew, it was in a big pot and there was plenty for everyone. She baked bread in the oven of that huge stove and she never burned it. The rolls came out golden brown and they melted in my mouth. Ruby's father, Jake, and her mom were special people in my life. They always treated me like one of their own kids. Jake had me ask for things in Athabaskan and if I didn't know the word, he taught me. He was one of the last members of the "small timber people" a band of Athabaskans who were the aboriginal occupants of the Tyone Lake–Denali Highway area. Dad drew Lily's flower patterns on the moccasins she made and she even made me a pair. Jake teased me all the time and told me we were eating bear if I asked, but it was really moose. Jake taught me Athabaskan phrases as well as individual words. His stories were about times of old when he and his tribe herded caribou into Butte Lake, a lake about 5 miles off the Denali Highway. I went fishing there with my brother on several occasions over the years. The stories of Jake's hunt were fascinating. They drove the caribou herd into the lake and then with boats, closed in around the caribou for the kill. They speared the caribou on the other side of the caribou closest to the boat. The wounded caribou couldn't thrash around and sink their boats with its hooves with another animal in between. The caribou were at a disadvantage in the water. Jake lived into his 90s and I loved visiting with him every summer until his death. Even when he was nearly blind and hard of hearing, he recognized me and I felt honored to have known him.

As I sat reading one day, Dad said, "Keep Frosty in the trailer while Mom and I are outside."

I admit I only half listened when he told me so when Frosty kept going to the door wanting out, I didn't give it a second thought when I let her out. I just figured she wasn't kidding and I needed to let her out or clean up a mess.

Dad yelled at me to come outside and when I did, he ran at me yelling, "I told you to keep her in. Why did you let her out?"

Faux Pas (Fopy) when he was about
5 weeks old.

———————————————————

I didn't know she was in heat and said, "Your dog is out. Why can't mine be out?" That was the only time I ever talked back.

The irony of it came soon after. Dad, supposedly watching her while she piddled one day, started working on something and forgot about her until he saw a husky hooked up with her. He chased the dog all over the yard but it didn't help matters any since the big husky dragged my little 18 inch tall dog all over the place. Dad finally conceded and let them finish the deed. Down the road, Frosty had three puppies. They were humungous puppies and the delivery about killed her. Dad killed two of the puppies because he didn't think she could nurse all three. We named the puppy Dad kept Faux Pas since the pregnancy was his mistake. Within two months, Faux Pas was three times bigger than Frosty and he continued to grow.

We were able to eat things other than our normal winter food when summer came. We only had canned fruit, canned vegetables, home-made sauerkraut, caribou, and moose meat in the winter. Anything other than apples in the way of fruit was a rarity in Cantwell. We saw watermelon at the store that summer and Mom bought a small one. It would have been a cull anywhere in the Lower-48 states, but we savored it even though there wasn't much flavor. The melon cost $12.

Mom was a good cook and her specialty was dessert. She didn't just make a chocolate pie. She made chocolate chiffon pies or rhubarb custard pies. She loved trying new recipes but she could only try things we had the ingredients for since our Cantwell store only carried the barest of essentials.

Butch and I rode to the store with Mom the day we bought that watermelon and while there, we saw a major Cantwell problem. One couple that I saw frequently in downtown Cantwell came to buy more alcohol. That day I saw the woman with her little baby boy in her arms and he was covered in blood. It wasn't his, it was hers from a bloody nose. She staggered into the store dripping blood all over her baby as she dangled him off to the side like a rag doll. We were all afraid she would drop him as she stumbled in. She and her husband fought regularly when they drank and there she was buying more alcohol.

Back then, alcohol was a real demon all over Alaska with the long winters. During one of the summers, a local man drove his car off the road, fell out of his car and drowned in two inches of ditch water because he was too drunk to pull his face out of the water. Two young people were decapitated in two separate car accidents because of alcohol and others in Cantwell died in drunken driving accidents. Some died from suicide. The stories were horrific and each loss a monumental blow to the community. Some of these people were people I knew and cared about and they died far too young. People died soon enough from other causes.

My teacher, Mr. Shoemaker, introduced us to a little culture that winter. He turned the radio station to the National Broadcasting Company every day after lunch. We lay our heads down on our desks and listened to classical music. I babysat his daughter Lynn whenever they went somewhere. They called her Precious Lynny Bug and she ruled the roost. The Shoemakers read the Dr. Spock book on parenting and believed that children had to express themselves any way they chose. If Lynn threw a temper tantrum, they didn't remove her, they removed themselves. Into the bathroom they went, to sit on the edge of the tub with the door closed until she finished with her tantrum in the living room. They called out to her; "Precious, are you finished?" and she would go into another fit. Later on, when they did finally put her in a bedroom for her tantrums, I witnessed her kicking the door and screaming until she was totally exhausted. One evening, before they left for an outing, she clipped the end of their dachshund's ear off with her little scissors. As the poor dog ran around yelping in pain and bleeding all over, they swooped Lynn up and said, "Oh Lynny Bug, you shouldn't have done that." I watched the poor dog in disbelief. In spite of it all, Lynn turned out to be a very nice young woman.

On November 2, Grandma Anne Nicklie's cabin in the village burned down. Her son, Johnson lived with her and when he made a fire in the stove, he poured kerosene on it to make it burn. Flames shot up and out of the stove and caught him in the face. Someone dragged him from the cabin but when he came to, he rushed back into the burning cabin for his dog. They found Johnson after the fire with the dog in his arms.

Sometime around this year, we lost a very nice man. Jake and Lily's son Alfred died. This tall, nice looking young man with a charming smile was gone. I felt a sense of loss even though there was a big difference in our ages. We had run side by side in the foot races the summer before. He took it good-naturedly when I passed him and just laughed when people teased him about a young girl passing him. Though it was unusual for Natives to invite non-Natives to traditional Native Potlatches, my family was invited because of the close friendship Dad had with Alfred. Alfred died on Dad's birthday and for years after, Dad visited Alfred's grave on Dad's birthday every year.

On the day of the Potlatch, people streamed in from other villages miles away to the Tansy's house. People talked at the Potlatch about the person not with sadness but with happiness at his life. There were ceremonial dances where they put on fur gloves and holding onto pieces of cloth, they danced in a circle chanting in Athabaskan. They chanted their songs, and danced the whole evening. I watched intently to the swaying motions of the dancers in the ptarmigan dance. It was a moving ceremony and I felt an ache in my heart for their loss. It just didn't seem right that this small community should have so many people dying before their time.

That winter colored movies came to Cantwell. Black and white "Ma and Pa Kettle" films were history. We loved our "Ma and Pa Kettle" movies because they were something to look forward to but when color came, things came alive on the screen.

My cousins came to stay with us for the summer that year. All of us kids moved into the hard-side tent behind the house with the boys sleeping on bunks and my cousin Linda and I sleeping together in a double bed. Butch told us ghost stories at night. He told a story about a mortician who cut people up and then tied body parts to lamp switches, which drove his wife crazy. She turned the lamp on in the dark and found a hand hanging off the switch. Butch always came up with the scariest stories and as we listened to these stories, we covered our heads with our blankets and begged him to stop. He climbed down from his bunk, crept across the floor and grabbed Linda and me by the feet. We both screamed every time and the boys all laughed. When we thought we heard him coming, he didn't, but when we gave up thinking he would come to get us, he grabbed us and pulled us off the end of the bed. We all waited for Butch's new story each night.

In the daytime, we played with the neighbor kids. Some of our neighbor kids were very mean to their chained dogs. When one of them broke his chain and came to us, we hid him. The skittish dog only came to us. We never wanted to give him back but my seven-year-old cousin Kenny caught him one day at the request of that family's son and handed him more than a dollar. When we found out, all of us were heartsick. We didn't feel that anyone should abuse their animals. Mom was so upset she looked for Kenny to spank him. All of us kids agreed that Kenny should not have caught the dog for the family, but we felt sorry for him so we made peanut butter and jelly sandwiches, and went to find him. The sandwiches were for him to stuff in his back pockets so the spanking wouldn't hurt so badly. Mom found the sandwiches in his pockets and then we were all in her bad graces.

Butch told us what practical jokes he and his friends played when he lived in Palmer. They targeted Hal, a younger boy for most of their jokes. They wrapped a dog turd in a Baby Ruth wrapper and gave it to Hal. He took a bite before he realized what he was eating. When the boys bought candy or pop, they ran to their clubhouse with it and Hal ran hot on their trail to ask for a share. If they gave it to him, he ran off with the whole thing. One day someone swiped a bottle of beer from their parent's refrigerator and the boys took off to the clubhouse to drink it. Knowing that Hal would be there soon, they gulped down the beer and peed in the bottle. True to form, Hal showed up and begged for part of the beer. As soon as he had the bottle in his hot little hands, he took off running and drinking it as he ran. He had about half of it down before the taste finally hit home.

I thought these were funny stories when my brother shared them with my Cousin Linda and me. We decided to play a trick on my cousin, Johnny, since he always wanted whatever Linda and I had. Linda and I covered some of our goat's turds with chocolate and handed them to him when he wanted some of our 'chocolate covered raisins.' He ate them and wanted more. Yuck! We tried it again by poking goat turds down inside an orange and giving it to him but he pulled the orange apart and saw the little gems. We were always looking for jokes to play on each other and then Mom told us of a joke played on her when she lived in Homer as a child. A friend of hers said she would make Mom pretty with makeup and instead painted Mom up like a clown with lipstick. They went for a walk and passed their cute teacher, Mr. Walsh. Mr. Walsh said hello with a big grin on his face and Mom didn't know until she passed a mirror later that day what her friend had done to her. Later, the girls decided the teacher was mean and dropped a cabbage down his chimney. The cabbage stuck and his cabin smoked up.

While the rest of us kids played, Dad went out east toward Paxson with the 6x6 to cut burned timber for the walls of our homestead earth house. He and Butch used the winch to load them onto the truck. Dad wanted burned timber because they didn't have to be peeled, they were as hard as a rock, and they lasted longer than if he had used regular trees. They hauled load after load to the lakeside. Dad put plastic up against the sand and then put logs up vertically for the walls of the kitchen. The underground room was habitable even with its dirt floor so we all, including my pets, moved out to the homestead. The raft that Dad built became our mess tent on the water. Mom and Dad slept in a small white tent on the shore, and the rest of us slept on the sand floor of our new underground room. I didn't mind the floor until the night a furry thing ran up and under my leg in my sleeping bag. I discovered that I shared my sleeping bag with a shrew. These little furry animals look like a small mouse with an orange colored nose. That's all it took for me to leap out of my bag and take off running. There were shrews all over the place. They were cute, but I didn't like the idea of one in my sleeping bag with me. In one night, my brother caught sixteen.

Building went on with a lot of noise and I lost Petie, my parakeet. I didn't know how he opened the cage door but he disappeared. Frantic, I ran all over the place looking for him and calling his name. One of my cousins found him in the underground room sitting on the new water pump for our well. He was hot and didn't like it in the sun where I had placed his cage. I had to give him away right after that because my parents said he was too much trouble.

My guppies didn't fare so well either. The summer weather in Cantwell can be very unpredictable. One day the sun shined and the next day it snowed. My guppies froze in their fish bowl on one of those nights. I had heard that fish can freeze in the winter and when they thaw, they are fine. No one told me that they needed to thaw slowly though. I set them on the little wood burning barrel-stove set up in Mom and Dad's tent. I didn't keep an eye on them and the next thing I knew they were boiling. They all had a proper burial beside the lake.

The lake we were homesteading on had a sand bottom and a sandy shore. On warm days, all of us kids buried each other in the warm sand with just our heads poking out or ran up and down the sandy areas of the beach barefoot to feel the warmth of the sand on our feet.

Jack West's liquor store burned that summer. I think he must have built a side room on to his store because I remember a side building filled with liquor. People hurriedly tried to remove all the liquor as the place burned and then a pickup backed up to the entrance and someone yelled for the men to load the liquor into his pickup so he could get it out of the way. They loaded his truck to the max and he drove away. No one knew the man nor did anyone ever see him again. As the man passed through, he probably thought it was his luckiest day. After that, Jack built a big, metal Butler building for the store.

Vacation Bible Camp came along and I wanted to go but Mom said, "No, you can't find your dress shoes so you can't go." When I found them, she said, "No, you can't go because your hair is dirty." My cousins wanted to go as badly as I did so they said they would help me wash my hair in the well water. Putting ice cubes on my head couldn't have been more painful. I had instant brain freeze from the frigid well water and my head pounded with piercing pain, but I was determined to get through it and go to Vacation Bible School for the week. We wanted to be around other Cantwell kids. None of us kids were used to being so far away from other people and now we were two and a half miles from anyone. Our perseverance paid off and at last, Mom finally said we could go.

When there weren't chores, we looked for mischief to get into. We couldn't stay away from the yellow jacket nest in the ground on the lake's edge. One of my cousins put a stick in the hole and then we all ran as fast as we could to get away when the yellow jackets, set on revenge, flew out. My little cousin, Kenny had short legs and was always the last in line on the path. He had the majority of stings but he always followed us back to the nest. My cousins went back to Anchorage at the end of summer and life slowed down.

When the Road Commission replaced the Nenana #1 bridge on the McKinley Park road and Dad heard the old timbers were available for salvage, he was right there to salvage them for our living room and bedroom walls. They were massive timbers at eighteen inches wide by six inches thick and up to twenty feet long. Dad and Butch worked for days loading and unloading the timbers. We had no fear of the sand caving in the walls of the living room and bedroom with those massive timbers nailed together with twelve-inch spikes.

Then the Alaska Road Commission notified Dad that we had to get rid of our goats since farm animals could not be on state property. The goats were our pets as well as our milk and we had had goats for three years. Dad couldn't bring himself to kill them himself so he asked one of the men from the Road Commission to come and do it. The man asked if Dad wanted the meat and we were horrified. That to us would be like eating our pet dogs. The man shot our goats and Dad decided it was time to stop working for the Road Commission. Since he needed to live on the homestead for ten straight months to meet his living requirement through the Homestead Act, he decided that it was a good time for him and Butch to stay on the homestead all winter. Mom and I stayed in our trailer in Cantwell for the winter. Dad moved the goat shed to the homestead along with tools, food, and bedding. That little shed became invaluable over the years since it changed from being his little getaway office, to taxidermy shed, to tool shed, to goat shed, to dog shed for sled dogs, to chicken coup. No building ever went to waste.

CHAPTER 5

1958

fall to fall

MOM ORDERED A CORRESPONDENCE COURSE FOR BUTCH'S SCHOOLING since there was no grade above the eighth grade in the Cantwell School. He snowshoed in once a week to pick up new lessons when winter set in. When he and Dad weren't building, he took that opportunity to go off on his own. He could have ridden with Dad on the school bus run, but snowshoeing in to Cantwell gave him exercise and a chance to have some alone time out of the cramped quarters of their one room underground dwelling. He and Dad had the timbers up for the back living room wall and the bedroom wall but nothing was habitable except the one underground room set up to be the kitchen. That winter, they poured concrete in the northeast corner of the kitchen for a very small bathroom, and I do mean small. It had a small shower, sink, cupboard, and a toilet. We held our elbows in as we turned around or we whacked them on the plywood shower stall. On the north wall of the kitchen, Dad put in salvaged cupboards from a torn-down house in Summit. He recessed a barrel for a refrigerator into the sand, in a horizontal position, on the south wall and built a door for it. It wasn't until I reached twenty-one years old that they bought a real propane refrigerator. Right in the middle of the room was a metal pole holding up the bracing timber in the ceiling. A coal chute slanted into the room on the west wall and that is where Butch slept. He nailed a board across the end of the chute to keep himself from sliding out of the chute at night. A small wood stove stood on the side with the cupboards. Dad moved in a big wood cook stove close to the cupboards. He mounted a fifty-five gallon cleaned out, metal, gasoline barrel on a 2x4 wood structure above the hand water pump to hold water and attached a water pipe running to the coal stove, sinks, and on into the bathroom so they could have heated water. Unfortunately, when we all moved in, there was never enough hot water for a good shower and the water just trickled out of the showerhead. The concrete floor of the shower stall brought the cold straight up from the cold ground and taking a shower was not enjoyable.

Cantwell had a shivaree for Mr. Gunther, my new teacher for the seventh grade that fall. They threw the Shivaree because he was German. The men at the affair hauled off his wife in a wheelbarrow and hid her. I loved seeing other people's customs. I remembered the wedding stories my aunt told me about the late 1930s in Anchorage. When a couple married, the neighborhood kids banged tin cans or tin tops outside of the newlywed's door until the couple opened the door and gave them money. As little kids, my mom and aunt were persistent when they banged their tin cans and never left before receiving their bounty. The couple paid to be left alone for the rest of the night.

Winter dragged by without Butch to keep me company. I actually missed him.

Occasionally I spent the night at girl's houses in Summit and I vividly remember one house in particular. I took a bath in a bathtub, with an abundance of hot water. The two sisters and I giggled half the night. In the morning, we went down to breakfast and there sat the girls' father NAKED at the table reading a book. Startled, I turned to leave the room when the girls assured me that everything was fine. They told me that their family had been members of a nudist colony in California and they still went nude indoors. I have to say, I never raised my eyes from my plate through that entire breakfast and I never spent the night again.

Approval for full territorial status came to Alaska in 1912 and on January 3, 1959, it became the 49th state. People had mixed emotions.

Some didn't want statehood because they said nothing could be gained by being a state except for more government interference. Our community would still be rural and we still wouldn't have police, a fire department, paved roads, city water, or sewer. Some thought statehood meant more growth and were happy at the prospect. At my age, I didn't care one way or the other. Life went on whether we were a state or not.

Mom babysat the teacher's daughter Lynn in the daytime and in February, Dad stopped by our house to pick us up and take Lynn home. Maggie, driving her uncle's jeep without a driver's license, came into our driveway on the wrong side of the road and hit our VW bus head-on. I was putting a rhinestone- embedded bobby pin in my hair and went hurtling into the windshield with the bobby pin still in my hand. Blood spewed from a gash near my hairline and as it ran down my face, it filled my eyes so I couldn't see anything. Lynn and Mom were fine but Dad had a small cut beside his eye. Mom lifted my hair to check the damage and assured me that I would be fine. Dad raced for our car and they drove me to the Summit nurse. She couldn't do anything but put gauze and a compress on my cut and tell my parents that I needed to go to Anchorage for stitches. Mom and Dad were up all night keeping me awake because they worried about a concussion. Every time I closed my eyes, they shook me to keep me awake. All I wanted to do was go to sleep. My head hurt but they couldn't even give me aspirin. We couldn't drive to Anchorage because the road closed for the winter so we had to wait for the 1 AM train. At half past midnight, we bundled up and headed for the railroad tracks. We had no railroad depot so people waited in their vehicles with the heaters on until the train whistle blew and the train rounded the corner. When Mom and I climbed out of the car, the bitter cold of the minus 40-degree night took my breath away and momentarily took my mind off my head. Once on the train, the conductor gave us a seat to ourselves and, wrapped in blankets, I settled in for a nine-hour wide-awake ride to the hospital in Anchorage. After x-rays and nine stitches, Mom and I went to Grandma and Grandpa's house and for three days, I stayed in bed because of my concussion. The car damage came to $345 and the hospital charges were more than that.

Dad took heart on Maggie and didn't call the State Troopers to report the accident. As a result, they ended up having to make payments on the bus repair and the hospital bill.

Since I was already in Anchorage, my parents decided that I should stay with my grandparents and finish the school year in Anchorage. Mom said later, that it was because the teacher picked on me but I don't remember that. I received good grades in his class and hated leaving my friends for the big city.

I settled into Central Junior High to finish my seventh grade. Coming from a small school of seventeen to a school of hundreds was a challenge. The kids teased me constantly because I blushed over everything. They wrote in the school paper, "Imagine what it would be like if Alicia wasn't blushing." I hated that I was so shy but my solitary life in Cantwell hadn't helped my social skills. I sat at the back of the class daydreaming of being back in Cantwell in our two- room school and with the kids I knew.

When school ended at the end of May, I headed home to Cantwell. It was nice to be back.

Dad and Butch worked hard closing in the bedroom area as well as working a little on the middle room. That room was eventually going to be our living room. Dad put up Mylar, a heavy plastic, on the cut out bedroom window openings. The plastic windows stayed until the late 1980s. The Mylar rattled with the cold winter winds and the windows frosted in the corners, but that was the best Dad could do with our finances.

He decided that the coal chute didn't work where it was. It protruded into our kitchen too much. He and Butch dug out another area beside the kitchen, put up log walls and that became the coal room. When a trainload of coal came in for us, the railroad dumped the rail car off on the sidetrack and we went to work. Dad, Butch and I shoveled a pickup bed full from the rail car and then shoveled all of it into the new coal room via the new coal chute. We were black with soot. It reminded me of when Mom told me that she and my aunt harvested coal from the shore in Homer for fuel when they were young.

Butch, at fifteen, looked older than his age. He had piercing blue eyes, sported a crew cut and even at his short height of 5'7" he was very muscular. He always had a winning smile and made friends easily. He was such a hard worker that a construction company hired him for the summer as a cement mixer. He mixed cement in a wheelbarrow and wheeled it to an area, dumped it and mixed more. Like the energizer bunny, he worked long hours on the job and then helped with the jobs on the homestead when he came home.

On the homestead, I pumped the fifty-five gallon barrel full of water every morning. My arms ached as I held on to the kitchen table with one hand and pumped with the other arm. I changed hands when my arm felt ready to fall off. I realized then how much water it takes for a family of four. If someone decided to take a shower in our slow trickling shower, I pumped the barrel full twice a day.

Once a week I did the family ironing. I put a heavy metal flat iron on the wood stove to heat up and then inserted a wooden handle into the top of the hot iron and moved it to the ironing board. We had two irons and one handle so when one cooled down, I picked up the other iron hot from the stove and continued ironing. I scorched several things when I first ironed with them. When we acquired a kerosene iron, I could adjust that one by turning a knob. I filled it with kerosene, pumped it up and lit it instead of switching hot irons. I scorched less with that one.

I also chopped kindling which I didn't mind unless I couldn't whittle down a hard log. I waited for Butch to come home so he could start it for me.

Washday in the summer was an all day affair. Mom and I dragged the Maytag wash machine outside, placed it on a piece of plywood in the sand, and ran an extension cord to it from the generator. We did the wash outside so the water spillage soaked into the sand instead of the floor. Dad only turned the generator on for washdays and some evenings in the winter, he turned it on so we could listen to music on the stereo. Once the machine was set up for washing, we heated water for the wash machine tub in buckets and then carried the buckets of hot water out to the machine. We also filled a galvanized tub sitting in the sand on the ground. That was the pre-cycle wash, which I had the misfortune of having to use. Each load had to be stomped for five minutes with a cone-shaped stomper. I always pleaded with Mom to cut the time down before my arms fell off. The water in the Maytag was so hot we used a wooden paddle to remove the clothes. Then we ran the clothes through the wringer and hung them on the lines to dry. If the weather was bad, it turned out to be an affair that went on for days instead of just one day as we checked the clothes for dryness day after day. Mom tried to plan washday around good weather, but it wasn't always possible. Our clothes had small, flying bugs clinging to them and were stiff as a board when we brought them in, but they were clean. Dad ended up buying a small wash machine for Mom a few years later so she could use it in the winter as well. There was a winter where friends of Mom and Dad's offered to let them do their laundry at the McKinley Park Hotel since these friends were caretaking the hotel.

Dad decided to build a log house above our earth house so he and Butch cut down trees and brought in several loads of logs. Butch and I were to peel them all that summer but when Butch went off on his job, I had to peel them by myself. I didn't like peeling logs because the draw blade caught on all of the sharp-ended branch knobs and I scuffed my knuckles. I labored at this task for long hours every day, and when I finished one log and asked if I could swim in the lake on hot days, Dad always said, "No, start another log." As I jerked the draw blade toward me stripping the bark away, I glanced at the huge pile of unpeeled logs. It didn't seem any smaller. I loved it when a big piece of wet bark peeled off in one long strip. Dad and Butch put some of the logs into the lake to soak for easier peeling, but it seemed that it took just as long one way or the other. One day, the inevitable happened. The draw blade slipped over a knot in the log and ran under my kneecap. The cut bled profusely but it wasn't that bad. I was back peeling logs the next day. Dad wasn't letting me off that easily.

I liked being outside because being inside meant being underground with no natural light coming in. We used kerosene lanterns when we first moved to the homestead. They just didn't give off enough light. Later, Dad put in copper tubing for propane lights that hissed all day and evening and in the winter as I sat studying, all I heard was the hissing of the propane lights. They didn't give off much light either. One time one of them caught on fire and a section of the kitchen ceiling burned since all we had on the ceiling was brown paper over the wood. We ran for the lake and hauled in buckets of water to extinguish it. Living next to water proved a blessing for our fire but it wasn't always a blessing.

Living next to water in Alaska also meant having an abundance of horseflies and mosquitoes and we had more than our share. If I swam in the lake, horseflies bit me on the back and mosquitoes were after me all day. Once Dad and Butch cleared some of the brush away from the house area, the mosquitoes subsided a little. The old prospectors used to call the vicious mosquitoes hummingbirds because of their size. I had bumps wherever I wasn't covered with cloth. Swimming in the lake was nice but going to a circus in Fairbanks topped that.

The Shiners' contacted families all up the railroad line about a circus in Fairbanks. They paid for all of the kid's fares to ride the rail and let us into the circus free. They also put us up at a school gym and fed us at the military mess hall. We were all beside ourselves with excitement. Mom and Dad said I could go but when I was given a big button to wear which said UNDERPRIVILEGED CHILDREN; my mom put the brakes on. She said, "No, absolutely not. No child of mine is going to wear a button that says underprivileged children. You can't go." I cried and pleaded with them in front of the other parents waiting with their kids. I even promised to take the button off once I boarded the train. Mom finally gave in and I left for Fairbanks. We didn't have much, but my parents didn't like the idea of every person on that train thinking we were poor. We met kids from other small communities along the railroad and got to go to a circus, a first for all of us. We had a grand time in the big gym with feathers floating all over from our donated, goose down, military mummy bags. Eating in a big mess hall with all of the military men was great fun. What the Shiners' did for the rail belt kids was awesome and I for one was very grateful.

When I returned to Cantwell from the circus, my allowance of seventy-five cents a week terminated. I wrote in my diary, "We're getting very poor." The effects of living on a homestead with only a small winter salary for income were even trickling down to me. We weren't the only people living on a shoestring though.

A family of five boys and their father came to spend the summer and winter in a tent in the Cantwell area. Mom invited them all to dinner. After the dinner of beans and cornbread, I walked around offering everyone a toothpick. Mr. Ault, the father said, "Thank you." I waited for him to take a toothpick and again he said, "Thank you." I was puzzled. I didn't know why he wouldn't take a toothpick when he said thank you. He finally gave me a big smile and he had no teeth. I thought it odd that Mom fixed beans for company until I realized why she had cooked soft food that night. Mom felt sorry for some of the boys that had no winter coats and she bought them some from the catalog. When it came to kids in need, Mom always reached out to help. It wasn't the first time she had reached out to help kids in Cantwell. When she saw that one little girl in Cantwell needed glasses, she bought them. When Butch and I visited the family in their tent that winter, we saw that all they ate day after day was fried caribou cooked over a pit fire in the tent. Butch and I felt sorry for them and cooked them up a huge pot of tapioca pudding, which the boys loved. This family migrated from New Mexico and we were astounded that they survived the minus forty degree temperatures of our winter in a tent. They made their way to Fairbanks after the winter and we stayed in touch for years.

A highway surveyor ran over our dog, Faux Pas that summer. We rushed him to Summit to see what the nurse could do but she wasn't able to help. We had no money to take him into Anchorage or Fairbanks so we waited day after day to see if he would make it. For the whole month of June and half of July, we nursed him as best we could and he miraculously pulled through.

Butch had a good friend at Summit named Daryl. They hiked the hills of Summit and found an old WWII plane, crashed on the mountaintop. They fished or just hung out together when Butch had time off. That summer Daryl drowned in Summit Lake. His family said he ate lunch and then went swimming. The person swimming with him saw him floundering and told him to hang on to his back while he swam them both to shore. Daryl hung on for a short time, then let go, and went down in the cold, murky lake. His swimming partner couldn't find him after making several attempts. Divers flew in from Anchorage, dragged the lake until the wee hours of the morning and finally found him tangled in some decayed branches at the bottom of the lake. They never did find out why he went down. When Butch heard the news, he went into the bathroom, threw up and then disappeared to grieve by himself. They were such good friends and it was a crushing loss to my brother. Our house was quiet as we grieved with Butch but building went on.

Dad and I went on dump runs to the Road Commission dump that summer. What some people thought of as garbage, my dad thought of it as treasure. Being so far from a city was hard when we were building because everything came in by rail. If a person forgot just one thing, they couldn't proceed until someone going into town on the train could bring the item back. Blazo fuel boxes we hauled home were used for shelves in sheds, shingles on the roof, flooring, containers for kindling, and the cans that held the Blazo fuel were used to cover holes in the roof. When we made these dump runs, we were always able to find something we could use for building. We even found live squirrels at the dump to take home for dinner.

There were ten dead grizzly bear carcasses in the dump when we went scavenging that fall. There was an abundance of grizzly bears and they were getting into people's caches of stored meat for the winter. The locals didn't tolerate animals stealing their food or breaking into their cabins. People didn't say anything when they killed one. It just appeared in the dump pile and the pile grew. Unfortunately, hides were not something we needed for the homestead.

Dad built our cache that summer. He and Butch used the winch on the 6x6 to maneuver the logs around. They lifted them up to the tall platform Dad built on top of the fifteen- foot long upright logs. He cut

This was the first picture of
our cache after it was built.

---

fifty-five gallon gas barrels in half and put them on top of each upright log to deter squirrels. When they finished the cache, it looked like a small log cabin on tall stilts.

They put window-sized screens where windows would normally be and then built the door. Dad put rails on the front side of the platform so no one would fall off. They then built stairs that could be hoisted up with an attached pulley so bears couldn't get into the cache. I don't remember the stairs ever being raised. Dad needed them down when he went to the cache several times a week to hack a piece of meat off a hanging carcass or collect some other stored food.

He peppered our caribou and moose meat to keep the flies away and keep bacteria from growing. It didn't keep them all away, but it kept the majority away.

Grandpa told me that when he was a small child in Flat, Alaska, they hung their bacon in the shed. When it grew a green mold, they just rinsed it off with vinegar.

Dad's cache was a real work of art, very sturdy and the biggest I had ever seen. Alaskans used caches mostly for winter meat but we used ours for other non-perishable foods as well. After Dad built it, I slept in it during the summer. I preferred sleeping in the cache to sleeping in the kitchen on the short little love seat. When earthquakes hit in the summer, which was common since Cantwell sits on a fault line, it was a bit unnerving since the cache swayed on the thin log legs. A few times, I headed for the door and down the ten steps to the ground.

After building the cache, Dad and Butch built a one- car garage.

When Dad wasn't outside building or fixing something, he looked for trees, either for kindling or for building. On one of his tree- cutting trips, his ax bounced off the tree and went through his boot and into his foot. He limped back to the truck and drove to the homestead while his boot filled with blood. When Mom pulled his boot off to check his wound, blood gushed from the foot. She tied a tourniquet around it until they could get someone to airlift him to Fairbanks. Within a few days, he was back cutting trees, but more cautious than before.

Dad guided for Keith Specking every fall and things were hectic at that time. Drivers trucked horses in and the hunters and guides loaded up their gear for the long walk into Dead Man's Lake. Sometimes a man rode a horse because of health reasons, but normally the horses only packed the gear.

One year when Dad guided, Mom took the wives, who had accompanied their husbands, in our old Desoto car into the park. We had purchased the car from the McKinley Park Hotel. She took them to visit a small hard- side tent camp run by a woman named Celia Hunter. It was a nice outing for the wives.

A Florida airport owner came to hunt that fall. He not only tipped my dad a large sum, but he sent my mom a piano and all the books to learn how to play it because of a comment she made about wanting to learn to play the piano. This same man helped pay for a Mouton (caribou calf- skin) parka, for me at Christmas and for a box of Florida grapefruit when I was in the hospital having my appendix out. The man was so generous that my whole family was overwhelmed with his generosity. A prince came to hunt one summer and brought his young wife. She was dressed in furs from top to bottom and had diamond rings on every finger. I thought she would be a snob but she very nice.

A benefit that Dad had as a hunting guide was that he sold his artwork to the hunters. His paintings held memories of their scenic hunt.

CHAPTER 6

1959

fall to fall

IN MID AUGUST, DAD SALVAGED A LOAD OF USED WOODEN SHINGLES from a house in Summit. He wanted the shingles to put on the roof of our garage. Butch and I climbed up on the roof and trimmed the shingles before we nailed them down. I watched my brother as he trimmed the shingles and then threw the knife sticking it into the roof. I thought I would follow suit, so I picked up his sharp knife, trimmed the shingle, and threw the knife. I hung on to it too long and instead of sticking it in the roof, I stuck it right into my anklebone. Blood ran out like an open faucet. Within two days, my leg was infected and swollen. Two weeks later, my brother and mother left for Anchorage so Mom could get Butch settled in with my grandparents for the school year. My leg worsened. I missed school because of the infection but Dad kept putting peroxide on it. When the redness faded and the hole looked better, he pulled the two raw edges of flesh together and stretched a Band-Aid across the wound. He put several more down the incision. I felt better about the butterfly bandage than Dad giving me stitches. It wasn't pretty when it healed with its one and a half inch long by one inch wide scar, but that's what people did with no doctor around. When we were sick or hurt, the first line of defense was to try whatever we had in the cupboard. Grandpa told me that's what my great grandparents did in Alaska during the early 1900s. They used chamomile or peppermint when they were sick with a stomachache. If they had a bad chest cold, his mom cooked up onions to put on his chest, and if they had a wound, they put glycerin and white iodine on it. They gave a constipated baby an enema by using the esophagus from a ptarmigan as a tube with a piece of macaroni at the end. They boiled onions with sugar as a cough syrup and used cornmeal mush plaster on the chest for pneumonia. They boiled caribou bones for tea when someone was sick and used mustard plasters when the gold miners had lumbago (arthritis) in their fingers. We had a little more up-to-date medicine in our cupboard like Vicks to swallow when we had a cold or peroxide that we used for all wounds. My wound healed and I was ready for school.

My new Texas teacher did as so many other outsiders did when coming to Alaska and seeing our bounty of animals. He decided he wanted to be a trapper. When he came that summer, he set his beaver traps in Fish Creek but didn't check them until the dead beavers bloated and were no good to anyone. Everyone talked about his lack of experience and it upset me because I hated the idea of trapping animals. Too many people moved to Alaska and thought of themselves as mountain men living off the land. I saw too many military hunters in our area shooting mountain sheep and caribou and only taking the head as a trophy. They left the carcass to rot alongside the gravel road. This teacher's beaver trapping experience reminded me of my grandfather's story.

When Grandpa was younger, he and his friend John went beaver trapping during the April 1929 beaver season. They were going to trap their limit of ten pelts, and sell them for $35 per pelt. John had a trapper cabin several miles from the railroad up the Chulitna River. With their homemade sled built like a wheelbarrow on skids, they boarded the train. With their supplies of food, two rifles, snowshoes, and the sled, they took the train to Caswell Station on the Alaska Railroad. From there, they headed up the river and traveled about five miles on snowshoes before they pitched camp under a large spruce tree. Because it froze at night and thawed in the day, they had a tough time keeping their wheelbarrow sled upright in the thawing snow. The webbing of their snowshoes stretched and broke, making it impossible to travel through the four feet of wet snow with broken webbing on their snowshoes. They were going to try patching them with willows on the second day but a moose happened along and they shot the moose instead. They skinned him, and cut the hide into strips that they used for their webbing repair. The third day, they took as much of the moose as they could carry on the sled and continued on to the river where they made better time with the sled on the slippery ice. They arrived at the cabin on the fourth day and cooked some of the moose meat. Grandpa said it tasted terrible because it was a spring moose and had not had much to eat during the winter. The next day they set ten traps and when they checked their traps, they found they had the feet of ten beavers. The beavers chewed off their trapped feet and swam away. Grandpa and John then changed their traps so the beavers were held under the water. They drowned instead of climbing out on the ice. After ten more days, they had six pelts.

John wasn't a clean person and after several days, moose hair covered the inside of the cabin from the shedding hide. Hair floated into their food, sleeping bags and coffee. Grandpa said he wanted to clean out the moose hair, but John said he deliberately put the hair on the floor to keep his feet warm. After 15 days, Grandpa fed up with the moose hair told John he was leaving unless John let him clean it up but John refused. Grandpa left with his three pelts, a slab of bacon, a few pancakes and a lot of moose hair in everything. He found a good place to camp on the riverbank that night and when he heard a crunch, crunch in the snow, it turned out to be John. He didn't want to stay alone in the cabin. In the morning, John said he knew of a shortcut to the railroad tracks. They had very little food left and they had to avoid traveling on the frozen river because it was melting so Grandpa went along with John's shortcut. Because the snow was melting, they didn't need their snowshoes. They could travel much faster without them. After

Termination dust on the mountains on a full moonlit night

a full day of traveling to where the railroad tracks should have been, they were nowhere in sight. Grandpa realized that they were lost. They ate very little that night so they would have food left for the next day. After wandering for three days and two nights, they finally heard the train whistle blowing and realized they had paralleled the tracks for two days. For two days, they chewed on the bacon rind. They couldn't catch the train when they heard it, but the section boss at Caswell Station picked them up on his hand rail car and took them to the section house where he fed them and gave them a bed for the night. The next day they flagged down the train for home. Grandpa and John broke even from the sale of their pelts after paying for their supplies and the rail fare. Grandpa told me what he learned from his trapping trip–he would leave trapping for real trappers.

Termination dust covered the surrounding mountains when school started. Early gold miners called the light dusting of snow on the mountains in the fall termination dust. Those that panned for gold in the summer usually terminated sluicing for gold at this time.

Only two of us were in the eighth grade that year, Nancy Anderson and me.

We were into a routine on the homestead and not much varied. There were no more Young People's Meetings for me. I went to school and then home to a quiet evening with Mom and Dad.

Winter hours were short and when it was daylight, it was only a light gray light like on an overcast day. Evenings came early. The sky was a brilliant blue against the white ground near the end of January, but prior to that, it seemed dreary to me. It didn't really matter if the daylight lasted longer though, since we lived underground. We usually spent our evenings reading in silence. I checked out books from the small school library weekly reading about all of the presidents and other people's lives. Mom and Dad bought me the Nancy Drew and Hardy Boy books as well as National Parks sticker books. I exhausted the school library and moved on to my parents books. Some evenings, Mom and Dad decided to listen to music and Dad started the light plant for electricity to the stereo. Most evenings they played opera. Dad sat down with the libretto and explained the operas to me as we followed along. The stories were usually sad which didn't help my spirits much on dark, cold winter nights. Some evenings, we had music that was more upbeat. When they played records from the musical hits, Mom knew every word and sang along with them. She had a beautiful voice and at one time wanted to be an opera singer. At the end of the evening Dad readied the house for night.

He banked the stove by putting in a shovel full of coal and bermed it so it burned all night. I stayed warm until the wee hours of the morning as I slept on the floor in the kitchen. Later, when I saw a spider on the floor, I slept on the little love seat in the kitchen. Mom and Dad had a wood stove in their bedroom and the unfinished room in the middle was an empty area, with a boardwalk between the bedroom and the kitchen. The middle room had no roof, doors or windows.

In the morning, Dad shook the grate in the kitchen stove to empty out the cinders and then added wood. Most mornings, he cooked a pot of hot cereal for us and covered it with butter and brown sugar. If he felt like making something else, it was usually pancakes. My favorite pancakes were sourdough pancakes made with a strong, yeast batter called starter. Taking the lid off the strong yeasty sourdough starter made my mouth water.

Every weekday morning Dad drove me to the crossroad where he turned to go to Summit on the bus run and I walked on to school. That is, unless it happened to be one of those whiteout days where I had to go with him to walk in front of the van.

On rare occasions when we were invited to someone's house for dinner, I was the designated dishwasher. As everyone rose from the dinner table to help with the dishes, Mom said, "Oh don't bother, Alicia will do them." I didn't mind washing dishes and I was fast so it didn't take long. What I did mind was that I missed some of the stories. I tore through the dishes and raced into the living room to sit off in a corner with a book and act as if I was reading while I quietly listened to their conversations. I was like a sponge with new material even when Dad wanted me to take different religious lessons.

He became interested in the Rosicrucian teachings and ordered lessons for me. Rosicrucianism started in the 1600s by a secret brotherhood of alchemists and sages. They believed in multiple lives and Karma. If a person did wrong to another person in this life, he would have this person in his next life to work out the wrong. That would be strong incentive to treat people right in this life. It was a comforting thought to me to think that I would be back for another life and wouldn't just die and be gone. Every lifetime taught lessons and made a better person. The teachings stated that a person could choose which lessons he or she wanted to learn in the next life. It was fascinating but I had just enough fundamental religion in my past to be confused. I questioned myself on what I really believed in.

Caribou on the lake.

In November, a whole herd of caribou lingered on our lake. The herd moved quietly over our frozen lake hour after hour. As they migrated, the stragglers trailed behind. I sat out on the snow bank silently watching the herd. The crunching of their hooves in the snow as they searched for dried lichen on the banks was the only sound I heard.

That was the same month Dad and I saw a gigantic colored meteor fall. We watched it as it appeared to hit the ground. Dad said he would search for it the following summer, but there were too many other things to do and he never went.

In December, everyone in our school had to take an eye test and everyone in the school flunked it. We all needed glasses. Studying under the dim lights of kerosene lanterns and propane lights didn't help.

Butch came home for Christmas and I didn't feel so alone. We snowshoed all over the hills surrounding the lake. He set snares for rabbits and hunted for ptarmigan, both of which he was always lucky enough to get. In the evening, I sat and talked to him as he skinned out the birds or rabbits. He told me about how school was going and what they did in the city for fun. When January came, he left. Mr. West left at the same time. After selling his store and property, Mr. West headed to Anchorage for his retirement years. Then I felt doubly sad to lose both of them.

There was a sense of anticipation to see what the new owners were going to do with the store. The first thing I noticed was a jukebox. The second change came when I saw magazines, comics, cards, parkas and mukluks on the shelves. I was excited about the new things and bought one of the first comics.

Dad decided to do some ice fishing to see if the whitefish would bit in the winter since they never did in the summer. We shoveled drifted snow off the thick ice to expose deep fractures in the crystal blue ice. He built a small fishing hut and we pulled it down to a small cove on the lake. After drilling a hole in the ice, he and I sat hour after hour trying to get just one tiny nibble, but nothing happened.

There was so little to look forward to in the winter and the one thing I really looked forward to was going to the movie at Summit. So often, Dad worked on the car engine on weekends. As Mom and I, ready to leave for the movie, walked to the garage Dad said; "We can't go; I just took the car apart." It upset us but we couldn't do anything about it. The vehicle was our livelihood and it had to be in good condition. It was always such a disappointment.

On evenings when I was bored and feeling as if I were all alone, I reflected on the stories Grandpa told me about my great grandparents.

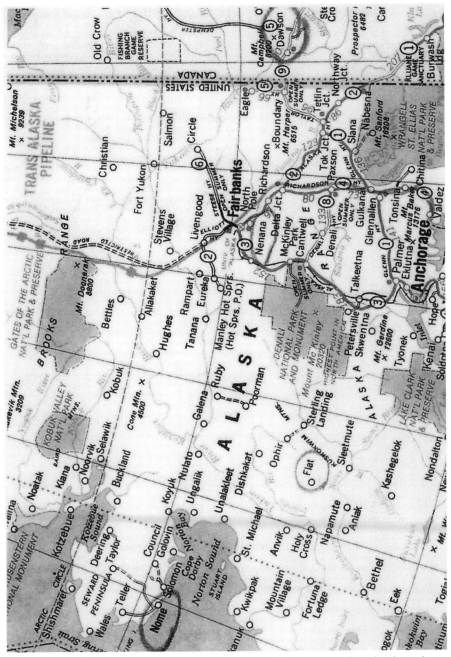

My great grandfather gold mined from Dawson to the area around Fairbanks and on to Iditarod and Flat.

My great grandpa, John Bagoje, changed to Bagoy in the US, came from a poor family of Austrian farmers who grew grapes and olives. After coming to America, he moved to Juneau, Alaska, to work as a powder man for the Treadmill Mine in the late 1800s. When the Klondike Gold Rush started in 1898, he headed for Chilkoot Pass and the Dyea Trail. He carried other people's supplies over the pass for one dollar a pound. He used this to pay his way via riverboat to Dawson and once there, he made a sizeable amount of money on his claim at Yonkers Creek.

After making a few other gold stakes in other areas, he took a short break and returned to Austria in 1906 where he met the woman he married. Unfortunately, the bank where he put all of his money collapsed and he lost most of his money. He and my great grandma returned to Alaska. They bought a grubstake of flour, beans, bacon, ham, canned fruits, a fourteen by sixteen foot tent and a pot-bellied Yukon stove from the Northern Commercial Company. They were the main suppliers of food and other goods. My great grandparents settled at Fox Gulch, outside of Fairbanks but found little gold so they moved on to Goldsteam, another place out of Fairbanks. That first winter, they lived in their tent at minus sixty below. They dug a shaft and then pulled out the dirt to look for gold. Mining was a slow process. They lit a fire in the hole every evening to thaw the earth. Great Grandma cooked on the Yukon pot-bellied stove in her rubber boots because the heat from the stove made a quagmire of mud on the tent floor. Every day she put down fresh spruce boughs to sleep on but by the next day, the branches disappeared into the mud from the weight of their bodies. My grandpa was under one year old and Great Grandma had to watch him closely. She also did the cooking and ran the windlass, a wooden handle attached to a log in a wooden cradle. They anchored a rope to the log and hung a bucket at the end of the rope. Great Grandma lowered the bucket down into the hole and when she turned the handle, the log rolled, thereby winching up a bucket of gravel Great Grandpa filled from the hole. She dumped the bucket of gravel in a pile for the sluice box, a box built like a trough that rocked back and forth. They washed water over the gravel to get rid of the large rocks and the small nuggets and gold dust settled to the bottom of the box.

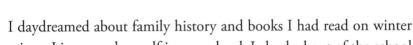

I daydreamed about family history and books I had read on winter evenings. I immersed myself in every book I checked out of the school library. After I finished one book, I mulled it over for a few days before I was ready to start another one.

Cantwell's winter temperatures dropped to minus forty and stayed there. Dad took the battery out of the van to take into the house at night and put it back in the next morning for the vehicle to start. Sometimes, he sprayed ether on the engine to start it. During that cold spell, he wanted some copper tubing for one of his projects. He said, "I'm busy so I can't go, but I want you to walk down to the store and see if anyone has any copper tubing." I wasn't thrilled with a four and a half mile walk in each direction especially when no one had any tubing. As I walked back in the cold and the wind cut into my cheeks like needles, I made deals with God as I quite often did. I promised, "God, if you will please get me home without freezing to death, I promise I won't complain when I have to do the ironing." If I was walking home from a friend's house in the summer, I vowed, "God, if you won't let a bear get me, I promise I will …" Within a mile and a half from home on the return walk to the store, a couple came along and gave me a ride. They chided me for being out in the below zero weather.

Four earthquakes hit within the same week in January. If people think it's scary being above ground in an earthquake, they should try it underground. The shock wave went right through the house and everything rattled. The walls even looked like they were moving.

As the boredom of a long winter lagged on, Dad thought I should cook some of the meals. One night I made meatloaf out of our caribou hamburger and I unknowingly used a rotten egg. Dad and I were sicker than sick but fortunately, for Mom she didn't eat any of it.

We bought our eggs in bulk and stored them small side down

in sand contained in a Blazo box. This way, they lasted better than three months.

The sun shone bright in February and snow glistened like diamonds. My spirits always lifted when the sun came back. Butch came home for a short three-day break and I stayed home from school to see him. We snowshoed for five miles on his second day home and saw sixty-five caribou and one moose. The only sound we heard was the crunching of our snowshoes in the deep snow and the squeaking of the leather bindings around our boots as we took each step. There were no prints in the snow but for our own, and it was so peaceful. As evening came on, the pink mountains turned blue.

Five days after Butch went back to Anchorage, a local man, motioned Dad to the side of the road. Dad, on his way to pick up the school kids, pulled over. When the man reached the bus door, he jerked it open and pulled my confused Dad out of his seat. Once out of the car, this man punched Dad in the face. He knocked Dad out, climbed on top of him, and punched him in the temple repeatedly. The teacher came along and as he tried to pull this man off Dad, he dislocated his own shoulder. By the time the teacher got Dad up and to the schoolhouse, Dad's head was two times its normal size and he looked like a disfigured alien. With the road to Paxson closed for the winter and the train on a shortened winter schedule, a local pilot flew the teacher and Dad to the Anchorage hospital. The pilots in those days landed right on the road if they didn't have skis on their planes. Dad's condition worsened and they feared a blood clot. Mom took the train into Anchorage on its scheduled day, which was two days later. I stayed home from school and kept the fires going since everything would freeze up in the minus forty-degree weather. Dad had infection in his head and everyone worried. After a week, he improved and Mom and he took a train back to Cantwell. Small communities had no police to intervene or calm raging tempers so people just had to work things out or kill each other. Being young, I wasn't privy to why the man beat Dad. Maybe it was something he said or unknowingly did. Long winters and cabin fever didn't always bring out the best in people. Dad healed and neither man ever said a word about it. They ended up friends again as people did in our small community.

We had an early spring that year and a portion of the lake thawed. Usually, when school ended at the end of May only a few buds appeared on what few leaf trees we had and ice still covered the lake. My friend, Nancy, came out for a visit from Summit and we untied the raft to float around the end of the lake. I poled with one long pole and Nancy poled the other side. The uneven lake bottom had pockets that

Most wolves are fatter than this one. He wasn't getting enough to eat.

dropped off to much deeper depths and when my pole hit one of these bottomless pockets, I followed the pole off the raft, into the frigid water and down into the deeper water where my feet didn't touch bottom. I didn't know how to swim and I didn't want to drown in the frigid lake so I thrashed around in the water and screamed. Nancy yelled at me to swim to the raft as it floated away, but I didn't know how to swim. She managed to pole the raft back to me and holding out the pole, pulled me in. I sat shivering as she slowly poled us back to the dock. Once I changed clothes and warmed up, we had a good laugh about my misfortune. The rest of the ice melted off the lake soon after that incident and summer slipped in.

Butch went to work at the service station in McKinley Park in June and I found myself alone again. Nancy only lived twelve miles away but I didn't see her or anyone else very often. Ruby and Maggie were my brother's age and they left for school in the winter. As time went on, we saw less and less of each other. My family was the only one living on the lake until 1962. Dad asked a friend to homestead across the lake and the man set up a trailer, but he didn't move into it until 1962. It seemed like the end of the world to a young girl.

When there were no chores for me to do, I withdrew to Icebox Canyon, an area a short way from the end of the lake. It was a small, beautiful canyon and I felt like it was mine alone. I walked over the animal trodden muskeg trail up the blueberry blossom covered slope to a thatch of near-dead trees. As I sat on the rock ledge of the cliff looking down on a dry riverbed, the world passed me by. If a breeze blew, I sat with my eyes closed and felt the breeze as it gently blew through my hair. I had a sense of peace as I looked over the surrounding snowcapped mountains and up into Icebox Canyon. One time, I took a piece of paper, burned the edges, and drew a mysterious map to nowhere on it. I did this after reading a Hardy Boy book and wanted the mystery of hiding a map. I wound my way down the bank onto an animal path that led to the dry riverbed and found a small niche in the rock wall where I hid my map.

A wolf pack lived up in the canyon and at night, we listened to their howling in the fall and winter. When I was at my favorite spot on the rock ledge, I always looked for wolves but they were never there for me to see.

Dad worked for Peter Kiewit Construction in McKinley Park that summer at a place called Sanctuary. In June, an operator accidentally dropped a load of creosoted logs on him and broke his ankle so they flew him into the Fairbanks hospital. Mom jumped in the car and drove out the road to Paxson, 135 miles and then on to Fairbanks, another 140 miles. She sent word back to Cantwell and someone lined up a truck driver to pick me up and drive me to Fairbanks. A friend offered to take our dog and I rode to Fairbanks with a truck driver driving his flatbed semi with a car strapped to the flatbed of the truck. Since Dad was in the hospital for several weeks Mom rented a room near the hospital for us. We didn't do much except visit the hospital, or sit in the apartment but it was a bit of an adventure for me to see something new.

When we returned to Cantwell, I went to Honolulu with another girl. That was a "big deal" with the local kids. As we waited for the one o'clock afternoon train, another person ready to board said, "Oh, are you going to Anchorage too?" I swelled with excitement and said, "No, I'm going to Honolulu." Honolulu, a railroad stop about an hour and a half down the tracks was where the north and southbound trains passed each other. The conductors traded trains there to be back home that night. It didn't cost much to take the little trip and it was exciting seeing new faces. The train had an open space between the cars and the tourists hung out of the open top part of the door to watch the scenery. There were just so many things for us to do in a short space of one and a half hours and we moved fast. We paid for our tickets and then ran through the cars to see if we knew anyone. Then we made our way through the bar car to see if anyone was playing a guitar, which they often did. We proceeded to the dining car, right past the bar, and gulped down a Coke. From there we hung out at the open area between the cars to let the wind blow in our faces and wave to anyone beside the tracks. The first stop was Summit, then Broad Pass, then Colorado, and then Honolulu when the conductor yelled, "Honolulu next stop." That's when we headed for the front passenger car. We loved it when people wanted to get off at a fishing hole or be picked up from one, because the ride became longer. When we arrived at Honolulu that day, the other train was already waiting. On the return trip, we settled down a bit and just looked for people we could visit with. At the end of the trip, we felt like we had been on a little vacation.

Dad met two couples on his construction job that summer. One couple came from Albuquerque, New Mexico, and the other couple from

Pinole, California. Both couples said they would be happy to have me live with them for the winter. Since no ninth grade existed in Cantwell, I knew I had to go elsewhere. The couple from Albuquerque was fun. They didn't have children but they did have a big, gray Weimaraner whose toenails were painted with robin egg blue nail polish. They told me, "We live in a subdivision with a swimming pool in the middle and we would love it if you came with us for the winter." I really wanted to go with them because I felt I would be special to them, but Mom and Dad chose the couple from California because they had kids. They had three little boys that Mom said I would baby sit as part of my room and board. They weren't leaving until the end of construction season which meant that I would be arriving late for school. I resigned myself to my parent's decision and waited apprehensively for our departure date.

My brother's twelve hundred pound moose.

Right after my birthday, Mom, Dad, and I went to an anniversary party in Summit for some friends. On the way back, a very drunk Cantwell man sideswiped our car and hurt my shoulder.

I healed, and within a week, I hunted with my brother who came home for caribou hunting. We left at 4 AM in cold rain. When Butch shot his caribou and then gutted and skinned it, I stuck my hands into the carcass. They throbbed from the cold. I wasn't the best person to take hunting because after he shot an animal and its death reflexes twitched,

I yelled, "Oh, no, he's still alive. Shoot him again!" He explained to me that the animal was dead because he shot it through the heart, but to appease me, he slit its throat. I loved going with him just to spend time with him, but I hated to see the animals killed. My brother always hunted successfully whether he hunted for ptarmigan, rabbits, caribou, or moose. He hiked all day if he felt there was a chance to put food in our cache. One time he shot a 1200-pound moose and he and Dad hauled it in with the 6x6 and used the winch when they hung it from the cache to dress out. On one hunt, Mom drove, I spotted and Butch slept since he worked a long shift at the gold mine that had reopened at Valdez Creek. He told us to wake him if we saw anything and when I saw a moose, I yelled, "Wake up, there's a moose!" Butch jumped up and out of the VW bus without even putting on his shoes. He shot but the moose ran into the woods and as he jumped back into the van he yelled, "Oh, God, it's the wrong side of the road to shoot a moose!" The law stated that the hunter had to kill the moose on a certain side of the Denali Highway. That was the only time he did not hit his game and it was a good thing.

CHAPTER 7

1960

fall to fall

Butch left at the end of August to spend the winter school year with my grandparents in Palmer. My host family and I left for California September 23 and on the 24th, the car broke down in the Yukon Territory of Canada. We towed a trailer and the axle broke just outside of Whitehorse. It took five days of waiting on parts to fix the vehicle. Towing a trailer over a bumpy, gravel, road with permafrost heaves and five people in the car stressed my host family from the beginning. At that time, the road had blacktop from Prince George to the Washington/Canadian border, but only gravel from the Alaska border to Prince George, British Columbia. The car repairs were just the start of trouble. We ate cherries one day and I ended up sick. Another day, I sat in the sun and had a bloody nose all over myself. Backseat riding always left me car sick. I left the window open a bit to breathe in fresh air and we choked on dust with each passing car. Each time I caused a problem, I was embarrassed to have caused these strangers grief. One night, a bear stole the caribou meat and the cooler that they were taking to California. We didn't hear anything. Somewhere along the way, Toni, the mother, called home only to find out that their hot water tank burst, flooding their hardwood floors and leaving water stains on the drapes. A laborer drilled holes in the hardwood floors to drain off the water and when we reached their house ten days later on October

4th, the place was a mess. Poor Toni was beside herself with three small boys, a young girl, and the house to get back in order.

I entered school and found everything different from my homestead life. As a homestead girl of fourteen I wasn't used to wearing dresses or curling my hair. Toni was a seamstress and in a short time she made skirts and a coat for me. The clothes were very stylish and even though my chopped off hair was not that stylish, I looked better than I ever had.

There were about a thousand kids in the school and because of my shyness, I didn't push myself to be outgoing and make friends. I was friendly but usually stayed in the background when there was a group. I was fine with a one on one but the mass of kids in the school intimidated me. Kids teased me good- naturedly. They asked me how big my igloo was and if I had a dog team that took me to school.

A girl named Sandy befriended me and we did everything together. She wore poodle skirts and loafers and seemed to be up on everything. She embodied everything I wanted to be from playing the violin to knowing how to fit in. I followed her like a shadow.

School presented problems for me because I was a month behind in the new subjects I was taking like Spanish and geometry. Geometry was so abstract for me and being behind didn't help. It wasn't just school subjects and a large school that I struggled with but home life as well.

It was nice to flip lights on and off at home and not have the constant hiss of propane lights. Throwing my laundry in the wash machine and dryer was something I didn't take for granted. Things were new and exciting but I was homesick and lonesome. I never felt that I fit into my new family's life. Toni showed me what she expected of me in the house with my laundry chores and babysitting but I felt in the way all the time. I felt like an intruder into their lives.

In October, Mom wrote a letter saying that the wine they made blew their caps in the bathroom closet and wine blew all over the inside of the closet. She also wrote that heavy snow had knocked down the telephone lines in twelve places and it took a week to fix them. That presented a hardship for the people in Cantwell since the Cantwell store had the only contact to the outside world.

I laughed at Mom's part of the letter about the wine caps blowing off and I read the letter aloud to Toni and one of her visiting female friends. Toni, incensed that I read that part in front of her friend, chastised me when her friend left. Having someone else's child under the roof who didn't know the do's and don'ts must have been a strain on her but I felt crushed with her reaction. I stayed in my room as much as possible or went to visit my friend Sandy.

Sandy and I walked downtown one day and when we passed a man who was shoddily dressed and a bit dirty, I said hello to him. He returned the hello and engaged me in a short conversation about the weather. Sandy stood off to the side and watched but didn't join in. When I left the man, she asked why I had talked to 'the bum.' I told her I said hello to everyone and he was a nice man. I felt that people were too judgmental because of someone's appearance. When we went into a café for something to eat, I observed another man who also appeared to be a street person. He ordered a free cup of hot water and an order of toast. When the hot water came with the toast, he squirted catsup into the hot water for a free cup of tomato soup. I sat watching him the whole time and I felt bad that he could only afford toast. It was the first time I had ever seen a street person and I felt overwhelming sadness.

Mom wrote again that they had closed in the middle room where they could now store firewood. In November, Dad put a roof on the middle room and built a Dutch door with the top and bottom opening separately. Dad cut the window areas out in the closed- in living room and put up Mylar plastic over the window openings. The Mylar gave a distorted image of the outside world being plastic, but light came in and that's what mattered. The middle room still had a dirt floor, but they took out the boardwalk to the bedroom. They didn't need to worry about snow in the middle room any longer. Mom's letters made me homesick as I navigated life in California.

Fog rolled into Pinole, California, and settled down to the ground in the wee hours of the morning. I curled my hair, but by the time the bus arrived at school, I had straight hair. I noticed that girls on the bus and at school went to school with rollers in their hair and then made a mad dash to the bathroom to unroll it before class time. Midmorning, the fog lifted and the sun came out. By lunchtime, kids congregated outside in the courtyard. Music blasted and some kids danced. Most of the time, girls danced with girls as the boys leaned against the walls of the school taking it all in.

Thanksgiving came and Mom wrote again. They wanted Butch to come home on the train, but they didn't have the $13.50 that it cost for the train fare so he had to stay at Grandma and Grandpa's. Dad rigged a radio antenna with a sucker rod in the ground and antennae in the tree. Now they listened to Sacramento and San Francisco on the radio every night. When I returned home, I listened to the world news and music from these far off places as well as the Trapline radio program relaying messages for people in the "bush" as the outlying areas of Alaska were called. I waited patiently through spells of loud weather causing static for the sounds of music to return.

In California, I dated a boy named Layman that winter. After we started dating (at school), five African-American boys grabbed him in the hall, beat him up and rammed him into the front of a locker damaging his eye. He had surgery and stitches on his eye and spent eight days in the hospital. A day after his beating, some African-American girls chased me but I managed to get to the bus before they caught me. I was confused and scared. I had never been around racial problems before, and I couldn't understand why these kids came after us because I didn't even know them and I wasn't prejudiced at all. Later, a Hispanic girl came into the bathroom, took one look at me and called me a "White bitch." Again, I didn't know her but she wanted to fight me. I grabbed onto the sink and as I looked into the mirror above the sink, I saw my face and it drained of all color. I felt dizzy, with ringing in my ears and my heart was beating so fast I felt it throbbing in my neck. She walked out of the bathroom and I stood holding the sink to keep my shaking legs from giving out. I didn't understand why these kids wanted to beat up on each other.

Mom's letters continued coming and I longed for my parents and

Me with my host family's kids in California.

Cantwell. Dad painted six pictures to take to Anchorage and place in Beirman's Jewelry and Gift store. Mom, convinced they would sell, made plans for the money, but when they took them in on the train, they sat in the store and didn't sell. Dad did a better job of selling his art to the hunters and his friends.

In December, Mom wrote that Dad started putting the logs up for the upper part of the house. When Butch, came home for Christmas, he and Dad moved logs with the truck. By the time he left, Dad and he had two rounds of logs in place. They dug all of the dirt off the roof of the middle room and kitchen to build the upper part. Working with the thirty-foot long logs, a winch truck, so few hands, and the extreme cold proved to be slow work. They pushed through the cold with their big parkas, heavy hats with earflaps, and heavy mittens with gloves inside. She also wrote that sending me to California was a mistake. She wrote that they were going to save the money to bring me home. My aunt checked airfare and the fare home was $128 from San Francisco. It took a long two months before they saved up the fare and I anxiously awaited every letter from home.

Mom's January letter was a sad one. Fopy (our dog Faux Pas)

disappeared in a blizzard at 30 below. Normally, he didn't go any farther than across the frozen lake so Mom and Dad worried when he didn't come back after they let him out. They called and called knowing that he would come bounding up to the door, but he didn't. The next day they drove east on the Denali Highway to check the teacher's traps fearing that maybe Fopy ran in that direction. The blizzard still raged and Dad slid off the icy road into the ditch. He walked five miles for help. Day after day, they waited for Fopy to come home, but he didn't. When Mom heard howling at night, they thought it was Fopy howling for help and they got up, dressed, and walked to the other side of the lake. No Fopy. Fopy always stayed right beside Dad when he worked outside and Dad really missed his company. There were fresh wolf tracks in the driveway a short time after he disappeared and they concluded that the wolves killed him and it was the wolves howling at night. None of us wanted to think of sweet Fopy dying like that.

February finally came and I said goodbye to my host family. I cried when I left my friend Sandy and, as a parting gesture, we tore a postcard in half and said we would each keep our half until we met again. We knew realistically that we would probably never see each other again. Finally, I headed back to Alaska to spend the rest of the winter with my aunt, uncle and cousins in Anchorage while I attended Wendler Junior High. My aunt was a very nurturing woman who loved kids whether they were hers or someone else's and she made me feel at home. Mom came in to visit for a few days and then I resumed my studies.

Mom continued writing once a week and the news in her next letter hit me hard. Mom and Dad canned forty-five pounds of caribou meat for summer. They had a new dog, part Norwegian elkhound and part wolf, named Nikka. My friend, Harold died. Ginny was dying with cancer (the woman who had me spend the night sometimes for their kid fix). Mom and Dad went to a movie in Summit and couldn't get out of Summit after the movie so a friend pulled them with his snow track Bombardier (a track vehicle for snow) to the railroad tracks so they could drive home the rest of the way. They were carrying eight kids now on the bus run from Summit and Mom drove the route most of the time. Ole Nicklie built a new house out of the village. The last sentence in her letter left me numb. "Frosty was having accidents because she missed you and we didn't want to deal with it anymore, so Dad shot her."

Devastated, I cried for a month every time I realized I would never see her again. I thought of how Frosty (I called her Pedi Rue) worshiped me and how lonesome she must have been. I held her on my lap all the time. I kissed her muzzle and talked to her. I was angry that my feelings never mattered when it came to my pets. Every loss of a pet made me vow that when I was on my own, I would take in every stray animal that came my way. I needed to take my mind off my little dog, so when the woman next door needed someone to clean her house, I took the job.

The first time I went to see the neighbor's house, I left horrified. Dried oatmeal spotted the floor and table, dishes were stacked for days, dirty diapers lay soaking in the toilet and the house looked like a tornado had struck. When I cleaned, I washed out the diapers, did the laundry, washed the dishes, cleaned the floors, and straightened the house. I loved a challenge like that and I did such a thorough job that she hired me to clean weekly. I loved it when she sang my praises to my aunt.

In April, I bought a little chameleon lizard from Woolworth's. Since it didn't come with instructions, I didn't know what to feed him. I tried hamburger but he wouldn't touch it. I collected dead flies from the windowsill but he wouldn't eat them. I fitted a little chain around his middle and pinned it to my sweater. Within days of buying him, I took him to school to show the kids. They were fascinated when he changed colors from green to brown. On the last period of the day, I went to my PE class and put the lizard in my gym locker. After our exercise, all of us girls showered, dressed and left for home. I dressed quickly; checking to make sure my lizard was okay on my shoulder. As I stooped over for my books setting on the locker room bench, a girl who had just come in from the showers rose up from grabbing her clothes. She came eye to eye with my lizard and let out a scream. Down she went onto the floor and into an epileptic seizure. Girls clustered around her as the teacher yelled for something to put in her mouth so she wouldn't swallow her tongue. Someone told the teacher about the lizard just as I headed for the toilet stall. The teacher bellowed out that whoever had the lizard had better get rid of it. I stood over the toilet in a panic but realizing that I couldn't flush my little lizard, I put him in my purse and unobtrusively left the building. In the following weeks, I knew that I was ill equipped to keep him and the store wouldn't take him back. They didn't even have food that I could buy for him. I knew he was starving to death and I felt he would have a better chance on his own. I finally put him on a bush outside of the house and prayed that he would make it. I don't think he couldn't possibly have survived the spring weather with its weather shifts. Life had such sad lessons and they were never easy.

Mom sent Butch and me money to come home for spring break and I was excited. It was the first time I had been home all winter. I couldn't believe all of the changes in the house and ran from room to room like a wild puppy sniffing out every new thing. Our stay at home was a short one but one that we all needed.

With the sun shining in May and the cold of winter receding, Mom's letters were more light-hearted. They bought a small aluminum boat as a surprise for Butch. Mom won $60 from the Cantwell minute pool ticket guessing when the ice went out on one of the rivers. She didn't buy the winning ticket though. She babysat a little girl and her father bought the ticket and wrote in Mom's name. Dad had more help with his building on the house from one of their pilot friends and they now had a cute kitten named Suki.

Since school was out, Butch and I returned to Cantwell on the train. We had a few days to settle in before going to work again. Butch dug out a pit in the floor of the garage, lined it with plastic, and Dad put up logs on the walls and ceiling so that he could stand while working under the van. Butch went to work at the Park. When he had time, he came home to help dig out the tunnel from the underground kitchen to the garage. The tunnel connected the two enabling us to go underground in the winter because the snow drifted to heights of more than six feet in front of our new front door. Butch said his arms felt like they were lead after digging that tunnel. Dad put up burned logs for the walls and ceiling of the tunnel and built a work place with shelves and bins at the tunnel end closest to the kitchen. At the garage end, he put up a massive door from an old discarded Road Commission freezer. During the winter, the tunnel radiated bitter cold and I hated using it when Mom sent me to get Dad for something on my winter trips home. In the summer, it was chilly and musty smelling. I still hated using it since there was just a little light at the kitchen end but then stark black the rest of the way down the tunnel. I ran as fast as

This was our underground kitchen. The door at the end went into the tunnel.

I could when I had to go. At first, they just had a regular door going from the kitchen into the tunnel, but eventually, they built bookshelves with trim onto the door. No one knew that a tunnel was behind the door and I loved showing it to my friends. THE HIDDEN TUNNEL BEHIND THE BOOKCASE. Eventually, they needed more light so they put up a door with a window. Light beamed in from the slanted skylight window Dad put in at the kitchen end of the tunnel and I lost my 'hidden tunnel.'

Mount McKinley view across our lake.

The new aluminum boat made life more interesting that summer. Poor Butch worked so hard that he didn't even get to use it. When I completed my jobs for the day, I took our boat out on the lake and rowed around. The only sound was the sound of my oars grinding in the oarlocks and the sound of the water dripping off my oars. If I didn't make a sound, ducks or loons sometimes landed close by. The sound of a scraping oar on the boat side caused them to lift off, scolding me as they flew away. The lake we lived next to was a mile long, 75-foot deep, sand bottomed, pristine lake. It was fed by a stream from the other side of the road. I came to know every nook and cranny of the lake. Tall rugged mountains cloaked in winter snow until mid June or later surrounded it. In the midsummer evenings, the mountains turned pink with the sunset and to me it was the most beautiful spot in the world. A gorgeous view of Mount McKinley stood white and tall across the lake. When the Russians owned Alaska, they called Mount McKinley "Bulshaia Gora," which meant big mountain. The Natives of Kuskokwim called it Denali, meaning The High One. At 20,320 feet, it was an awesome mountain.

A gentle breeze blew much of the time in the evening so I put the oars in the boat oarlocks and lay back letting the summer sun warm my face and the breeze take the boat wherever it wanted while I daydreamed. If there was no breeze, the mosquitoes pestered me on my trip around the lake. The terrain at the lake differed from the terrain two and a half miles away at the Road Commission. Aspen trees and ferns covered their woods. At the homestead there were very few trees surrounding the lake, and even fewer aspen trees. The ground, covered with muskeg (tundra moss) and lichen, felt like walking on a soft bed. It was so soft that it was hard to keep my balance or pick up any speed when I hiked. Short blueberry bushes, black crowberries, and low bush cranberries also covered the ground around the lake. Across the road, tall black spruce trees grew. Labrador tea and willow bushes covered the surrounding area of muskeg around the marshy edges of the stream. Trees harbored a waterway, which made a natural refuge for the summer Trumpeter swans and ducks. Beavers, muskrats, and foxes were in abundance. A fox den hid in the trees across the road from our driveway. If I closed my eyes, I smelled the willows and the menthol smell of the Labrador. The depth of the permafrost in the area discouraged strong ground cover and aspen trees. Anything growing on top of the permafrost had a shallow root system. This frozen ground went to depths of 68 feet in some areas on the homestead. Tundra ponds held surface water on top of the permafrost on our property across the road. As I rowed along the edges of the lake that summer, I noticed fish carcasses around the shoreline. This mystified me since we couldn't catch the fish with a fishing line. When I asked Dad about it, he said he thought someone set off a DuPont spinner (dynamite) sometime before we moved out to the lake.

About midway through the summer, Dad put a set-net out in the deepest part of the lake. He rowed out, flung the net with its buoy line off the side of the boat in the morning, and then rowed out to take the net in that evening. I cleaned the whitefish caught in the net. Some days there were none and other days there were as many as eleven twisted up in the net. Even though the net was not the perfect answer to catching white fish, it worked better than trying to catch them on a hook. The fish wouldn't bite on a hook when they could eat a generous amount of vegetation on the bottom of the lake.

I worked at the new Cantwell Store Café waitressing, cooking and washing dishes. They didn't have much on the menu so most of the time I just cooked hamburgers. I took a picture of my first dollar earned at a real job and sent the film in for developing. The next thing I knew, I received a letter from the FBI asking why I had taken an illegal picture of currency. I wrote a letter explaining things and waited for them to come take me to jail but nothing came of it.

The view across the lake.

One day at the café, I met a woman with a very flat nose. We were the only ones in the café. We talked and she told me that she had had an abscessed tooth in the front. She didn't go to the dentist when it first abscessed and when she finally went, the abscess had rotted her nose bone. They scraped it all out and put a plate in her nose. The plate went straight down at one height. I think she told me so I would never let a bad tooth wait. The next winter, this woman and her husband returned to Summit late one night when their car stalled. She and their baby stayed in the car while her husband walked on to Summit for help. She saw a bright light which became brighter and brighter. The light seemed to be getting bigger and it finally dawned on her that it was a train. Their car had stalled on the tracks and with the blowing snow and pitch-black night, they couldn't see where they were when they stalled. At the last minute, as the realization dawned, she grabbed the baby, lunged from the car and flattened herself and the baby into the cut out snow bank beside the rail. The snow bank was seven feet tall so there was no place to get completely away from the train. The train whistled through the narrow snow corridor embedding her in the snow berm from the shear pressure. When the train hit the car, it skidded down the tracks for quite a distance until the engineer could stop. This woman was incredibly lucky. Neither the baby nor the mother had one scratch.

The only excitement that took place in downtown Cantwell that summer occurred when the only horse in Cantwell waited outside the store for unsuspecting people to come out with groceries or ice cream. The horse, owned by a local family and let go to survive on his own, learned that he might find food at the store. As people departed the store, he grabbed whatever he could out of their hands, be it ice cream or a box of food. If he couldn't scare the people into dropping their food, he head- butted them and became very pushy. Kids were an easy target if they had ice cream. Kids with ice cream learned to run when they left the store. Ads, a kindhearted man from down the railroad tracks fed him apples when he came to his door. We all felt sorry for him but didn't know what to do about him since he belonged to someone and had to fend for himself. He managed to survive for a few winters on his own with people giving him whatever they thought he would eat. After a few years, he disappeared. I assumed that he either starved to death, or the wolves or a bear killed him. Again, I was left to question the way people treated animals.

Not a lot went on that summer, but Mom, Dad and I did take a trip to old Denali at Valdez Creek, a distance of 70 miles east of Cantwell on the Denali Highway. Denali, the gold mining area from the late 1800s, had some very interesting buildings, and it was Mom's favorite place to go. We waded through two streams to get to the old mining town and as we trudged through the brush, we happened across old buildings hidden by vegetation. An old hotel or bunkhouse with a six-foot coffin in one room and some other old buildings sat hidden in the thick, tall bushes. There were still things lying around such as old inkbottles, rusted old tools and even an old rusted gold pan. It felt somewhat eerie walking through the buildings. I tried to visualize how it had been in that age-old mining era when it was crowded with miners. History steeped itself in the Cantwell and Valdez area. Every little piece of junk in this ghost town stimulated my imagination. I conjured up stories that might have gone with them. Every broken piece of anything seemed priceless to me even though the broken pieces were worth nothing to anyone else.

Swollen Creek was Valdez Creek's original name because mosquitoes bit the first prospectors to the area so badly that their eyes swelled. Later prospectors renamed the area Valdez Creek.

My friend, Jack West told me how John Carlson discovered a 52-ounce gold nugget in 1904 at Valdez Gulch. That brought in more than one hundred gold miners to work placer mines in the same area. After them came the McKinley Gold Placer Company from New York. They bought claims that men lost because they couldn't pay their bills. That's when Carlson thought about building a roadhouse and store beside the incoming railroad tracks. He invited Jack to be his partner and once they started the store, the mining company bought their supplies from the store. The supplies were sledded to the mine and it started a good business for Jack and John.

Prior to the railroad, horse drawn sleds and packhorses sledded in all of the supplies for the Valdez gold mining area from Chitna, 250 miles away. When the railroad came, the Alaska Road Commission opened a sled road from Cantwell to Denali. The road cut the distance the miners had to travel for supplies to seventy miles. Once the Alaska Road Commission built the bridges on the Denali Highway, the route became much easier. Back then, it took packhorses three days to go the seventy miles. They also used dog teams when some of the early prospectors hired on with Carlson and ran their dog teams with supplies and mail to the mining area.

When I was younger and the men sat around Jack West's stove, they each tried to top another man's story. Some of the stories were just bragging rights and some were good history. They talked about the mining methods in those days when they used canvas pipe, sluicing boxes and some hydraulic equipment. With the hydraulic mining, they used canvas hoses to run high- pressured jets of water to dislodge rocks and sediment from the ground. To mine by hand, they used picks and shovels.

Natives from Copper Center and other villages set up camp on the other side of the creek from the miners at Valdez Creek. They hunted, fished, and then sold some of their meat and fish to the miners. Some hired on with the miners and mined a small claim of their own.

The Natives moved from Valdez Creek to Cantwell to work on the railroad and later they hired on with the Alaska Road Commission to work on the roads. Long before Caucasians came to the area Natives traveled through the Cantwell area every year for their hunting trips, but they had no permanent residences in Cantwell until they moved to be near the railroad. During the war, the railroad, short on laborers to repair the rails, hired Cantwell Native women to work on the rail as Gandy Dancers, a term used for railroad track workers. They worked as hard as the men did with their picks and shovels.

We only went to Valdez Creek once that summer, but the memories of it stayed with me.

Hunting season opened and people geared up for the season. Mom and Dad's pilot friend Chuck flew a hunter off the lake for a bear hunt when his plane hit a short tree at the end of our lake. If the water wasn't chopped up enough by revving the engine and going from end to end to churn the water into waves, the water sucked onto the pontoons and held the plane down. That's what happened that day. Chuck revved his engine and gunned the plane but the water didn't let go of the pontoons until the last minute and when he got to the end of the lake, he went up in the air a little but not enough to clear the tree. When he hit, his plane cartwheeled onto its back and we all ran to the end of the lake. They pulled Chuck and his passenger from the plane. Luckily, they had only minor injuries.

CHAPTER 8

1961

fall to fall

FALL CAME ON TOO FAST AND IT WAS TIME TO LEAVE THE HOMESTEAD again to go to school. Butch boarded with our deceased father's widow Leola in Palmer and I went to live with Grandpa and Grandma. Both my brother and I were in Palmer for the winter.

I was born in Palmer and even though I made friends, I found it hard to make close friends. All of the kids grew up together and had formed their circles already. I went to school with most of those same kids at a younger age but they didn't remember me. As soon as the boys saw how easily I blushed, they were relentless. I was disgusted with myself to be in high school and still not be able to control my blushing. Boys winked at me over their lunches and sat grinning at me after they finished eating. I couldn't handle it and resorted to eating my sack lunches in the bathroom for the first month until I met girls to eat with. The boys liked me and didn't mean anything by their actions, but they just loved playing practical jokes knowing I would blush. They put a prophylactic in my book when I went to sharpen my pencil, and then they laughed hysterically when I discovered it.. When it happened, I turned to a girl across the aisle and asked who put the balloon in my book which made them laugh all the harder. I was so naïve about life. I felt like I was one step behind in everything.

THEN I HAD TO GET GLASSES. I always sat at the back of my classes but then I couldn't see the blackboard. The glasses lasted only a short time after someone on the bus yelled, "Look! She has four eyes." After that, I removed them on the way to school and squinted from the back of the classroom or asked someone next to me for chalkboard information.

Grandpa was old school and whenever I received a phone call he barked, "State your business and get off the phone!" It didn't give me much of a chance to build relationships with friends or boyfriends. I had never had phone access before, but having him scold me when I was on the phone embarrassed me.

We lived far enough out of town that I seldom had company. I loved to stay in my small bedroom and read since I wasn't into television but Grandma worried about my reclusive nature and knocked on my door often to check on me. Then she insisted that I come out and watch television with them. Sometimes I did, but usually I begged off and read. Whenever I spent the day at home sick, I watched her soaps with her but I found if I was sick three months later and watched the shows, they hadn't changed much since I last saw them.

Grandma had such a sweet smile and a quiet reserve that no one would have guessed she was a worrier.

Her generation came up with the 'clichés,' "What will people think?"

"Make sure you have on clean underwear."

"What if you were in an accident? "

"Think of the starving children in China."

She lived in fear that I would end up pregnant as so many of the small town girls did and she wasn't going to have it happen on her watch. She kept a tight rein on me. It was just Grandma's way to nag at me, but soon I developed an ulcer. Grandma had her own burdens other than me because at the same time I lived with them, my great grandmother was also with them.

Great Grandma, a very bitter woman talked all the time about how her nephew stole all of her money as well as her pig. She received a $4,000 inheritance from her father, and her nephew offered to put it in his home safe for her since the depression scared people away from banks. He spent it all and she couldn't prove it was hers because she gave it to him with no proof. When her pig wandered onto his property, he kept the pig and wouldn't give him back. She never let her resentment go and as a result, she became more bitter with age.

For the last seven years of her life, she lived with Grandma and Grandpa and was so different from Grandpa's loving mom and dad. They were adventuresome, hard working people who loved their kids. Grandma's mom feared everything. She hated the mountains and thought they were going to fall over and she hated the water they lived next to for fear of drowning. She was grouchy all the time. When she came out of her room, she always chided my uncle and me for something.

The doctor said he wanted to see my Mom so she took the train to Palmer. He told her that she needed to remove me from my situation because my ulcer would get worse if I didn't move. Mom wasn't happy about my moving but she asked my stepmother if I could also board with her for a total of $130 a month. My stepmother agreed and I moved in with her, my three half-sisters Diana, Norma and Pam, and my brother.

Once I moved in, my brother informed me that I couldn't call him Butch anymore. The other kids in school called him his given name of Dave and he liked it. That ended the Butch era. He hated it if someone in Cantwell called him Butch, but after all those years, changing his name was hard for me. If I slipped up in public, I got a dirty look from him.

Dave (Butch) had already spent a year in Palmer and he had a social life. He rarely stayed home. On weekends, he worked at a resort on the lake as a dishwasher and the stories he told me made me sick. His instructions from the cook were to take all of the uneaten pickles, olives, and peppers off people's plates and put them back in the jars. The cook also instructed him to rinse off the uneaten lettuce leaves decorating the plates. He worked at the restaurant for a couple of months and then quit. When he wasn't out with his friends, he worked on the car he bought. Dad chastised him for spending too much time working on his car but he loved the car and it was hard for him to leave it alone. I needed money and didn't want to sit home so I found a job.

I ironed. Two older women I ironed for wanted everything ironed on their mangle, a piece of equipment with a foot pedal for raising and lowering the top of the heating element. To me, it seemed a cumbersome way to iron small things. I ironed their bras, panties, sheets, everything that I didn't think needed ironing, but it was a job, and I didn't complain. I also ironed for a family of seven. When I ironed for them, I went for the day to iron two huge baskets of clothes. First, I sprinkled and rolled each piece. I couldn't iron the wrinkles out without watering them. I took no breaks and only made fifty cents an hour but I felt a sense of accomplishment when I finished those baskets.

The husband of this family went bird hunting on the Cook Inlet mud flats a year later. He became stuck in the quicksand mud and couldn't break free. As he slowly went down, his friends, lying on their bellies and reaching out, pushed the rifle barrel into his mouth so he could breathe through the barrel but they couldn't save him. He went down and the tide came in before they could do anything else.

Being in Palmer again brought back memories of my early years in Palmer. I was born in a small downtown house in Palmer. I remembered sledding down Snodgrass Hill at seven and going to the Center Theatre on weekends to see Tarzan movies. Back then, we had a newsreel, cartoon and the movie all for twenty-five cents. An old Collie lay in the lobby and I always stopped to pet him. At Christmas time, all of us kids went to the theatre where Santa handed out stockings filled with oranges, apples, nuts and candy. We sat in our seats waiting for someone to call our row to the stage for our stockings. At Halloween, we all trick or treated at the stores where we received large candy bars.

The best memory I have of that period in my life came in knowing Mr. Walker. He was a tall, thin, elderly gentleman who always greeted us kids at the door of his small shed-sized cabin as though he expected us and seemed genuinely glad to see us. He treated us like little adults and we loved it. His jug of malted milk tablets never ran out even though he gave each of us one every time we visited. We treated them like lifesavers, sucking on them until nothing remained. It was always fun visiting his tiny dwelling behind our trailer. About four of us at a time crowded in to sit on the edge of his tall, built in, single bed and listened to his stories of the Grand Old Opry. His little cabin had everything in its own place. His bed nestled on the wall to the right of his door. Ties in every color hung above the bed. Dozens of ties, one on top of another bulged from the wall. I marveled that they didn't spill down on us. Above the ties sat a shelf for his treasured violin, which he took down at our request and showed us how to play. A small wood stove with a metal mobile hanging above it whirling round and round with the draft skirted the wall straight across from the door. On that same wall, was a little window with four small panes of glass. The wall to the left of the door held a long overhead cupboard and the wall with the door held up short shelves holding bunches of letters, small knick-knacks and the container of malted milk tablets. A little table with one chair sat in front of the stove and all of that filled the small cabin. I loved the small cabin with its miniature furniture. It was just right for a small girl. Every year at the same time, he went south for a few months to play with the Grand Old Opry. The days weren't as much fun without him.

Now, here I was living in my birth town again.

One weekend, we were all sitting around bored when Dave said, "Why don't you give me a perm?" I knew I could read directions on the Toni box and I agreed to do it. Dave had straight, blonde hair and quite a few of the popular movie stars at that time had curls or wavy hair that they combed back into a wavy ducktail. My sisters giggled when I rolled his hair on the rods but he acted as if it didn't bother him. He only wanted the front of his hair done with three curls. It turned out great. His friends and the girls at school liked it so much that one of his friends came to me to have his hair permed as well. They didn't want anyone to see them as I curled their hair on the rods, but a few behind the scenes pictures were taken.

On another weekend, I wasn't feeling well and my stepmother told Dave to stay home and keep an eye on me. Dave really wanted to go somewhere. He asked, "Will you be alright if I leave?" I told him I would and he took off like a shot through the door. About an hour later, I doubled over in pain. I called my stepmother and she came home to get me. The roads were icy and she crept down the road at 10 MPH because she was afraid she would slide off. I threw up and when we arrived at the hospital, I was throwing up bile. Hospital personnel knew my appendix had ruptured. They called the doctor but he came in drunk. They hooked him up to oxygen and it took a while before he sobered up enough to perform the surgery. He cut a jagged three-inch incision to remove the appendix but didn't put in a drain tube for the bile that seeped into the cavity. A week later, I returned to school and didn't realize what a terrible job he had done until the next time I had surgery. That doctor had a serious drinking problem. Four years later, he died in a drunken driving accident.

Mom's weekly letters made me homesick. Mom and Dad saw three wolves, two black and one gray on the road and then saw another two on the bus run to Summit. There were hundreds of caribou around the homestead. They were roaming from the homestead to the bluffs a mile down the road. Dad went into Anchorage and the hot chimney on the bedroom stove caught the wall on fire. Fortunately, Mom put it out with a fire extinguisher. Dave and I hadn't been home all winter and Mom said in her letter that she wanted us home for Spring Break. That gave me something to look forward to and I counted the days.

Sometime during this period, a horrible incident occurred in Palmer. John Bugge, an old Palmer homesteader, died. His house and barn sat on a large piece of land where a Carr's grocery store now sits. Mr. Bugge homesteaded his land in 1915; my aunt even knew him in the early 1940s when she was a child. He had some of his fingers cut off on one hand and that freaked my aunt out but he was harmless. His only quirkiness came from his love of cats. People dumped off cats until it was estimated that he had more than ninety at his place. When he died,

The house from the front.

the authorities closed the cats in the barn and burned it to the ground. Again, I was sickened at how people disposed of animals.

Mom's March letter said that there were caribou all over from Cantwell to Summit. I missed seeing the caribou migration each year. She went on to say that Dad had finished the log work on the upper part of the house. It didn't have any windows or doors yet, but the logs were up and the roof was on.

Dad studied books on building log houses to glean ideas and each book offered different ideas. Since he had never attempted anything like it before, the project seemed overwhelming. First, he winched each log into place with the big cable winch on the 6x6 truck. Then he chain sawed and chiseled each large, round log to fit snugly against the previous one. He dished out an area near the end of each log for the cross over log. Hours were spent on each one putting it in place and then honing it down to fit just right. It wasn't as easy as building with the Lincoln logs kids used to play with. Lincoln logs were uniform and easy to assemble. Before placing each one in its final resting place, he put insulation between the logs. To hold the logs in place, he nailed 2x4s vertically to the bottom logs to hold the new log in place. He drove twelve-inch spikes into the logs with a sledge- hammer to anchor everything once it was complete. After all the logs were up on the walls, he cut the window holes, fireplace hole and door hole. It sat unfinished

Dad and Oley Nicklie
working on a project.

---

and even when the upper part was used in the early 1990s, the fireplace still wasn't built. A board covered the opening.

While walking to downtown Palmer that spring, my grandparents pulled up and told me to get in the car. They were on their way to the hospital to say goodbye to Great Grandma. She died before we arrived. I knew I should feel sad for her but I really felt that she had gone to a place where she might be happier.

We didn't go home for spring break because of finances but when the end of May came, Dave and I headed home. I felt torn. I loved Cantwell but when we left the sunny days of Palmer, we knew we were headed for Cantwell where summer was one month behind. Ice still covered the lake and snow still covered areas of the ground. I reset my brain for winter again.

Dave worked at the McKinley Park service station again. The manager, pleased with my brother's work, told my parents. They told him that I also needed a job and he gave me one. I worked as a maid in the hotel where people came from all over the world to spend their vacations. That impressed me. THEY WERE FROM ALL OVER THE WORLD.

My work partner was a young high school exchange student from Kenya, Africa. We were unlike the other maids, who took until the train came in at two to finish their hotel wings. We worked well together and finished our wing by noon, swapping chores from room to room to keep the job from becoming monotonous. The hotel presented me with more history.

———————————————|■|———————————————

Construction of the hotel started in 1937, and it opened in 1939. The Alaska Railroad owned it. In the beginning, the tours into the park were in two Alaska Railroad buses. Before the war, the military tested winter equipment like cold food rations, clothing, stoves, tents, parachutes, and boots in the park. In 1943, the military used the hotel as a recreation site for military men. It had eighty-seven rooms and became a relaxing place for the military men to take their seven-day furlough.

The wagon that sat in front of the old McKinley Park Hotel.

———————————————|■|———————————————

An old wagon sat out in front of the hotel when I worked there but I didn't understand the relevance of an old wagon. I thought wagons were only associated with the old west. When one of Mom's friends brought her an old wagon wheel from an overturned wagon at Valdez Creek, I learned the importance of wagons in Alaska's mining history. They used wagons to ferry supplies to the gold mines.

The old McKinley Park Hotel closing up for the winter.

It was nice living in the employee dormitory with the young college women on the top floor and the college men on the bottom floor. A floor mother and a floor father monitored our floors making sure that no one crossed the line. A narrow boardwalk ran between the dormitory and the hotel, and when employees finished work, they normally left the hotel to hang out in the dorm. At mealtime, we all gravitated back to the hotel employee's dining room via the boardwalk. If a good movie was playing in the basement theatre, I went.

Because work was all we had to do, after we finished working, I walked the trails in the woods. One day, I walked to the post office at the railroad station when I spotted a cow moose and her calves. Alaskans know better than to mess with a cow moose that has calves so I veered off the path to give her a wide berth. Two elderly women coming down the path were headed right toward the moose and one said to the other, "Look at the horse and babies, Claire." I shouted at them that it was a moose, not a horse and that they needed to turn around and go in the other direction. I anxiously watched the moose as her ears shot straight back showing her anger. The women heeded my warning and retraced their steps.

Mom drove to the Park to visit on some weekends and sometimes she picked me up to spend a night at home. She called from the Cantwell store leaving a message that she would come for me on my day off. I loved going home even though I had to sleep in the cache on a narrow Army cot. It was exciting doing something different from the day-today work and it gave me a chance to catch up on the news. We almost started into a war with Cuba, and I didn't even know it. That was nice because I didn't stress about anything. Grandpa always said the reason he liked working out of town on the roads was that work was all he had to worry about.

On one of these weekends home, Dad gassed the VW when Suki, their little cat, rubbed against Dad's leg, purring as she rounded his leg and then passed under his gas can. At that moment, the filled gas tank sloshed out at the lip of the tank and spilled down on her. She let out a shrill "eowl" and took off running. We chased her down and Dad ran her into the lake to rinse her off. She avoided him for days. Normally, she brought presents, i.e. mouse parts, to Mom and Dad and deposited them on the rug beside their bed, but they had a break from those visits.

On another weekend, Nikka chased after a porcupine and received a slap in the face from the porcupine's tail. She had quills in her face and some in her mouth and I had the unpleasant task of removing them as she yelped in pain. I held her down, clipped the ends off the quills with scissors to release the pressure and pulled the quills with pliers. I fought her all the way, but I won and she trotted away quill free.

Dad decided he wanted a dog team the following winter so he started collecting dogs. He didn't care if they were good runners or not. He just wanted a dog team. Homer Nicklie gave him a big malamute husky named Danger. Dad added another dog to the team by trading one of his paintings for a beautiful Samoyed husky puppy they named Winnie Pooh. One day in early winter, she disappeared and when Dad tracked her, he found wolf tracks joining with her prints. He followed the tracks all over the countryside but couldn't find her. Two days later, she came back by herself. It was unbelievable that they didn't kill her. That is the only time I ever heard of a dog returning after an encounter with wolves.

CHAPTER 9

1962

fall to fall

I EARNED A TOTAL OF $269.80 AT THE HOTEL THAT SUMMER. I RETURNED home for my winter clothes, boarded a train for Palmer, and prepared myself for my junior year of high school. That year I went without my brother and I moved back in with my grandparents. Grandma and I vowed to make a better go of it, and we did with the strain of having Great Grandma gone.

In September, my brother and a friend hitchhiked Outside on the Alaska Canadian Highway. Alaskans used the term Outside for going to the Lower-48 states. They headed for Minnesota and college at Mankato State University but lost their ride in Edmonton, Alberta Canada. Hitching another ride to Montana, they then hopped on a freight train to Minneapolis. After going without food or water for thirty-one hours, they jumped off the train and picked some field corn. Their feast of green corn gave them diarrhea. They planned on hitch hiking the rest of the way, but were ticketed in Minnesota for hitchhiking on a freeway. We Alaskans learned the hard way. They rode a bus the rest of the way and Dave said the whole trip cost $11.50.

Right after I received the letter from my brother about his travels, I received a letter from Mom about their happenings. They put an oil stove in the bedroom. Dad wouldn't need to load the stove with coal every night to last until morning.

Here I am in the all girl drum corp. I am the one in the front row, fifth from the left.

Mom's October letter read that the middle room was finally ready for a floor and by the time I was due home, Mom said they would have the floor in and have furniture built. For four years there had only been the two rooms with an open dirt floor room in between. Building took time because everything cost money. I loved hearing about the improvements on the homestead but I didn't think too much about them since I had filled my time with activities at school.

I joined Mr. Plumbley's All Girl Drum Corp and came out of my shell even further. Mr. Plumbley reminded me of an ex-marine barking out his orders, "No chewing gum! Spit that gum out! Nothing looks worse than seeing someone chomping on gum!" We all knew how he felt about gum, but a few girls forgot occasionally. I don't chew gum to this day. He barked orders, which was a little intimidating to me, but he just wanted us to stand out as an excellent drum corp and we rose to his expectations. Sixteen of us played during half-time at the Palmer basketball games as well as during a few basketball games in Anchorage. In our senior year, we even took first place in the Anchorage Fur Rendezvous Parade. We froze in our new outfits of short kilts, berets, long stockings and capes that didn't cover much. Trying to beat a snare drum, do a fancy little step, throw sticks in the air, march on icy streets in regular shoes, and sidestep the horse manure from the horses in front of us was a challenge. Even though we wore little white gloves in the parade, our fingers were so cold we could hardly hold the sticks and drum at the same time. Catching the sticks after we threw them three feet into the air tested our ability under duress. We were a close bunch and we laughed and shivered through all of it. My legs looked like a plucked chicken's legs with all the cold bumps I had even though I wore nylons under my knee- high socks.

I joined the Future Nurses of America. One or two days a week I donned my candy stripped outfit and went to the hospital where I took ice water to the patients, delivered meals and ran errands for the nurses. I loved it because I felt needed. My life was going well.

I didn't really have many clothes for school, but I gave the illusion that I did. I made up a monthly list of all my clothes. In the evenings when I didn't want to watch TV or have a good book to read, I put my clothes together in outfits on my list. I switched items back and forth to look like new outfits thereby stretching my clothes out for a month with my different combinations.

I acquired a small circle of close friends by my second year in Palmer but I felt that everyone in the school was my friend. One boy asked to walk me to classes every day. I wasn't interested in him as a boyfriend, just a friend. No boys asked me out for quite a while and I wondered why until someone told me that this boy threatened every boy who was interested in me. Some of my brother's friends had a strong talk with him to correct the situation in my brother's absence. One of my brother's friends showed an interest in me and me in him. He wanted to date me the year before but my brother said, "No way!" As Bill questioned, "Dave, you know me. Why can't I date your sister?" my brother replied, "BECAUSE I know you!" Well, my brother wasn't in Palmer now and Bill asked me out. Grandma called for permission from Mom because I was only sixteen and Bill was twenty and out of school. Mom said okay and let me date him. He was a perfect gentlemen the whole time I went with him.

Most of the time Bill worked on his 1957 Chevy or drag raced down one of the back roads to a place called the Butte. I watched the races when I could but that wasn't often. We went to movies and the school gave me permission to invite him to school dances. The first year I dated him, Mom said I could date him for one evening on the weekend. Sometimes I was allowed to have a date with him in the daytime on Saturday or Sunday as well. Even though we could only call it a date on those days, he was allowed to pick me up after school so I didn't have to take the bus. The girls sighed with envy over my getting to ride in his shiny salmon and white Chevy, but I wasn't impressed with cars and could have cared less what he drove.

One day in the spring of my junior year, he asked me to drive his car home while he went somewhere with a friend. I didn't have a license, but he assured me that if I took the back street, I wouldn't get caught. That wasn't so with my luck. I drove so slow that a police officer followed me.

When he pulled me over, he asked, "Whose car is this?"

Everyone in Palmer knew who owned the '57 Chevy.

"It's my boyfriend's car."

"Why are you driving it?"

"He wanted me to take it home for him."

"May I see your driver's license?"

"I don't have one."

"May I see your permit then?"

"I'm sorry officer, but I don't have one of those either."

The officer gave me a warning with a note attached that I had one week to get my driver's license. I went into a panic as I wondered how I would explain this to my grandparents. I told Grandpa. Surprisingly, he wasn't angry. He put up cardboard boxes in the yard to teach me parallel parking and I practiced in their car. I didn't really master backing in to a parking spot. When we went down the drive, Grandpa explained, "Mitme, good drivers never have to use their brakes. They slow down before they get to their stop."

After studying the instruction manual and practicing all I could, I went for my driver's license at the end of the week. I took the written test, and then the officer and I headed out to the curb for my driving portion. I slid into the driver's seat of grandpa's automatic car and waited for the officer's instructions. He walked to the back of the car and told me to step on my brakes to check my lights. I had already put it into reverse to get out of the parking spot and I nervously stepped on the gas instead of the brake. The car shot backward as the officer jumped out of the way. He must have had prior experience with that mistake. It shook him up though, because he leaned his head down into the passenger side window and said, "Turn off the car and step out, please." He invited me to walk to the Frontier Café for a coke or a cup of coffee. I'm sure he made the offer to calm both of us. I completed the driving part and did well except for the parallel parking. He told me to work on that part.

When the Drum Corp accompanied our basketball team to Anchorage, we always stopped for dinner at the Mountain View A&W Root Beer Drive-In, located in a suburb of Anchorage. The fast food drive in had an old, shaggy African lion in a little cage on wheels in their parking lot. I always had a heavy heart when I saw him because kids teased him and I even saw people throw lit cigarettes into his cage. Every time we stopped, I looked at his sad eyes and felt like crying. That poor lion lay in that cage in every kind of weather and every kind of teasing for years and years.

Bill went into the Army Reserves. When he left, he said, "I don't expect you to just sit around while I'm gone. Don't wait for me." After a while, I dated a little. I didn't feel comfortable dating several boys at once, although that's what Grandma wanted me to do. She thought that was safer than dating just one boy and getting too serious.

I went home for Christmas and as I sat hour after hour on the long train ride home, I counted dead moose on the tracks. There were more than one hundred. Every winter it was the same thing. Moose stood on the railroad tracks or the roads to get out of the deep snow. Every year, there were dead moose lining the tracks and roadsides. The railroad crew may have picked up some of the moose for the Palmer orphanage, but they weren't picking up all of them.

I thought back to when I was younger and how much I enjoyed this train ride as I flitted from car to car. Now I sat on the hard, naughahide

Me, standing in front of the
partially completed upstairs
part of the house.

---

seats staring out the window and listening to the rhythmic clack as the
train cars passed the joints in the railroad tracks. I enjoyed watching the
scenery of grand, white, snow covered mountains in the distance and
frozen steams with spruce trees shrouded in deep snow. Occasionally, a
white hare darted back and forth through the trees or a fox stood beside
the tracks watching with abject curiosity as the train lumbered past. If I
didn't see the animals, I saw their tracks as they criss-crossed each other
over the frozen terrain. A young woman boarded the train at one of the
stops and sat down across the aisle from me. We talked about anything
and everything to make the time pass faster. It was always the same on
the train trip home. If he or she departed sooner than my stop, I felt a
momentary sadness that I had lost a newfound friend. On several occasions, we promised to keep in touch but we never did. We didn't have
access to all of the means of communication that we have today and
though we lived on the same rail line, we never saw each other again.
On this trip when I reached Cantwell, we bade each other farewell and
she waved from the window as the train pulled out. We never saw each
other again.

This hare was standing on my snowshoes.

Dave was homesick in Minnesota even though Mom and I wrote him often. He wrote to me telling me he wished he could start his college experience over and do everything right. When he first arrived at school, he left his admittance cards and one of his books for his classes in a friend's car. The friend left town and Dave had to acquire new ones. We were both used to a small town and he was having a hard time adjusting. He made friends easily, but things were overwhelming. His grades weren't good and he feared he would disappoint Mom and Dad. He felt guilty all the time and in every letter, he expressed it. I didn't know how to answer. I wrote drivel about how my winter was going.

My winter passed smoothly. I loved the evenings when Grandpa turned the TV off and company visited. Grandpa told stories of old-time Alaska. He stories were about gold mining days in Iditarod and Flat.

In 1910 when the big gold strike hit, my great grandparents and grandpa boarded a stern wheeler which took them down the Tanana to the Yukon River to Holy Cross and then on to Iditarod. Grandpa said Iditarod was a mosquito infested hell hole. There had been strikes at Otter Creek and then discoveries on Flat Creek, Willow Creek and other tributaries.

Great Grandpa John built a log cabin and chinked it with tundra moss. My great-aunt Doris was the first baby born in Iditarod and she was born in that cabin. They started a water-hauling business but soon the townspeople moved a few miles away to better gold mining areas.

This was my great grandparent's first roadhouse at Otter Creek near Iditarod.

A man offered to sell Great Grandpa a roadhouse on a gold stream called Otter Creek which was ten miles out of Iditarod. It had twelve rooms as well as a bar and eating area. Great Grandpa bought it and Great Grandma cooked meals, made desserts and homemade bread for the miners. Up to forty men ate at the roadhouse daily. This location became known as Discovery Otter. Grandpa told me that it wasn't all work there. The town celebrated the Fourth of July in a big way.

The festivities included things like a tug of war between mining crews, running board jumps, old men's races, women's races, women's nail driving contests, fat men's races and pie eating contests. The kids had doughnut eating contests and mule races. They also celebrated birthdays, Thanksgiving and Christmas.

Great Grandma gave birth to another daughter, my great aunt Mary and the work load was overwhelming.

Grandpa at Discovery during the gold rush

Riley Investment Company was the largest mining operation in that area. The owner, George Riley, was a crooked man and claiming to own all of the property in that area, he ordered Great Grandpa off the property.

My great grandparents moved and lost all of their investment in the property.

They bought another roadhouse with a bar and soon Riley again ordered them to move off his property. This time Great Grandpa refused and told him the roadhouse was his and he wasn't moving again. Riley's men, the Discovery Boys, descended on the property and washed all of

Flat, Alaska during the gold rush in 1911–1912.

Discovery/Iditarod about 1911 — Great grandpa's bar and rooms are on the right.

the earth from beneath the roadhouse with their dredging equipment. The entire roadhouse fell off the bank into the river. All of the liquor, bar equipment, furnishings, and personal things floated down the river. They were left with nothing.

A friend, who was a mining operator and saloon owner, gave Great Grandpa an opportunity to run his bunkhouse and bar in Flat and Great Grandpa took it. The friend, Jerry Ford, struck it rich and gave the establishment to Great Grandpa.

Grandpa told me that the miners paid their bar tab in gold dust and cash. As the men poured out gold dust from their pouches, some fell into the cracks between the bars counter planks and at the end of the evening, Great Grandpa swept it into a pan.

A man who had cut firewood all winter for Riley's operation shot Mr. Riley because he refused to pay the bill. The woodcutter was taken to Fairbanks, where he was tried and then hung.

Great Grandma had another girl, Great Aunt Eileen.

When the people voted Prohibition in, Great Grandpa sold the bunkhouse and bar in 1917, and purchased a six-acre farm with a house and a huge greenhouse. The greenhouse did well with the hot, long daylight summer days and they sold produce to the miners, families, and ladies of the night. Then they acquired chickens and a cow someone left behind.

Grandpa said that as a small boy, he fed the cow, rinsed out the liter beer bottles for milk, cut grass for the cow and delivered the vegetables, milk and eggs to the people. The miners called the row of prostitute houses 'The Line.' Grandpa talked often about walking 'The Line' to deliver food. He said he and the family ate powdered eggs and saved the chicken eggs to sell. Great Grandma even made gelatin from boiling the hooves of reindeer.

Once more bad luck hit the family. An early run off on the river in the spring of 1918 caused the river to flood. Water came up over the ice, flooding the banks, washing out the farm, root cellar and greenhouse. It about took the house. The Yukon Gold Company sent men and equipment to save the house that sat filled with two feet of mud.

Great grandparents and family in Flat 1916.

Great Grandma had just gone through a traumatic time saving the life of six-year-old Doris who was badly mauled by a huge Malemute Husky and this setback seemed like the last straw. It wasn't though because they put the house on skids and moved it to higher ground.

In order to rebuild, Great Grandpa went to work for the Yukon Gold Company and at the same time cleared more land. He hired a little one-eyed Irishman called "One eyed Jimmie" to help him and he began to rebuild. They built another greenhouse and enlarged the house. The cupboards were made of gasoline boxes with pretty draw curtains that Great Grandma made. The kitchen table was mess hall size made of shiplap. A bench held two dishpans for washing and rinsing dishes. Two twenty-five gallon butter barrels were used for drinking water. They had a wood stove with a chrome- plated front, a round card table and chairs in the living room. There was also a homemade easy chair stuffed with rags and burlap and covered with pretty material. A large homemade bird cage had several canaries in it that Great

Grandma bred and raised. There was a long shed connecting the out-buildings to the house and greenhouse. They used it as a place to store firewood, use as a milk shed, and washroom. A hand crank washing machine sat in one corner. In the back yard, they had an outhouse, dog kennels, a root cellar and cow barn made of logs.

Great Grandpa and Grandpa hauled water in five- gallon cans using a shoulder yoke. In the winter, Grandpa hauled the water by dog team from Cottonwood Creek. By the time he reached home, the water was frozen solid and he rolled the barrels into the house.

A Mr. Twitchell with his Laplander reindeer herders drove the herd to Flat each winter and supplied the town with fresh meat, which was scarce. Great Grandpa allowed them to butcher their meat on the farm and in exchange, Mr. Twitchell allowed Great Grandpa to choose a reindeer from his herd for his own. Great Grandma made sausage, headcheese, pickled tongue, and sweet breads from it. Nothing went to waste.

On these drives, the Lap women followed the herd with their children and supplies. Their sleds were shaped like small boats and a reindeer pulled each sled.

One winter, Great Grandpa roped his pick of the reindeer and when he pulled it into the barn, it head butted him and pinned him against the wall. Grandpa had to hit it in the rear with a shovel to get it to back off.

Great Grandpa and Grandpa took gold pans and shovels and sniped for gold in the summer of 1919. They came upon a large circle of Alder brush standing out from the rest of the surrounding area. Great Grandpa thought it might be the remains of a dump- site left by previous miners and began digging. They took out several dollars worth of gold. They built sluice boxes, started digging in earnest, and took out about twenty to thirty dollars a day worth of gold. Soon a U.S. Marshall showed up to tell Great Grandpa that he was digging on Yukon Gold Mining property and had to leave.

That same year Great Grandma had my great aunt Gabby.

Great Grandpa heard about a platinum strike in Good News Bay in the summer of 1920. He went prospecting with a friend but they didn't know what the mineral looked like and overlooked it. They about drown and came home empty handed.

When Grandpa told me these stories, it dawned on me the reindeer herd brought to them in Flat each winter was the same herd that was herded to Cantwell in 1920 from Good News Bay.

In 1921, Grandpa was 13 and the family decided he needed to be in Anchorage to attend a high school. They tried to sell their farm and property to no avail. Great Grandpa came up with a novel idea. He sold five- dollar tickets for a house drawing and sold enough tickets for the five kids and two adults to travel to Anchorage. They left Flat with two trunks, two barrels and two suitcases. Transportation from Flat to Iditarod was an old Model T flatbed truck mounted on wooden railroad tracks. It ran five miles an hour. At the banks of the Iditarod River, they boarded a gasoline launch called, *Sea Wolf.* Benches served as tables, beds and chairs. For two days, all they had was pancakes. They reached Shageluck Slough and boarded the "St. Joseph", a Catholic missionary boat, for their next leg. There were staterooms on that vessel. Grandpa said the mosquitoes were thick. After a day and a half, they reached Holy Cross. For seven days, they waited for transportation. There were no accommodations for travelers but Grandpa said the Natives were kind and offered an empty cabin. They also shared their ducks, geese, fish and Indian ice cream with the family. The SS Seattle III finally arrived and they boarded. There were staterooms, a large dining room and a social room to read, play cards or dance in to an old Edison phonograph. They made twenty miles a day, stopping to load wood along the way to burn in the boilers. Once in awhile they ran aground and it was hours before they were free. They finally reached Fort Gibbon, which is now called Tanana. From there they caught the "General Jacobs" which went down the river to Nenana. They also went aground in several spots. It had taken them thirty days to reach Nenana.

The rails from the Anchorage end and the Fairbanks end were not connected yet and it was going to be another thirty or more days before they would connect. Great Grandpa's money was running out and winter was coming on. He met up with a teamster, Dave Patterson, who was driving the Tote Road, the gap between the rails. He drove a team of four horses and agreed to transport the family across for three hundred dollars. The family boarded a work train of box cars and flat cars for a four hour trip to Healy where there was a construction camp and roadhouse. After an overnight stay in Healy, another train with flat cars loaded with lumber and supplies took them another ten miles to the end of the tracks, which ended two miles north of McKinley Park. They shared a leaky barn for the night with the horses. After breakfast, they were back on the road behind the four- horse team hauling a freight wagon, driving precariously over rough and muddy roads. Great Grandma and four girls rode in the wagon while Great Grandpa and Grandpa walked the railroad grade wading through streams and mud all the way. Where the bridges weren't finished the wagon bounced, swayed and wallowed up steep inclines through the Nenana Canyon. It was frightening. One barrel of possessions not properly tied on, slid off the wagon going more than a three hundred foot vertical drop into the river. When it became unsafe for them to stay on the wagon because of the hazardous road, Great Grandma and the girls had to walk. When Great Grandpa and Grandpa were walking the right of way approach-ing Riley Creek at McKinley Park, they heard "fire in the hole" and before they could get out of the way rocks fell all around them. They were bruised and fortunately, that was all. That night, they slept at the railroad section cabin at Windy. The next day it snowed and snowed on them all day as they walked to Cantwell. They spent the night at Cantwell and again the railroaders housed them. The fifth day of their journey it was dry and easier to walk. They arrived at Broad Pass where the track started again. The work train and two coaches travelled twenty miles an hour. The grade was soft causing the coaches to uncouple from the engine at times. Each coach had a pot- bellied coal-burning stove. After eight hours on the train they stopped at a place called Deadhorse where there was a roadhouse. Nellie Neal, the owner, charged Great Grandpa double for a filthy barn and terrible food. They pulled into Anchorage October 5, 1921.

My great grandparent's first house and greenhouses in Anchorage.

The old time Alaskans were so strong. Nothing stopped them. They didn't whine about their losses. They just moved forward. After listening to Grandpa's stories, I always felt pride at the family's resilient nature.

I went home for spring break and Dave was home from college. Mom and Dad went to town and since Dad's young friend Walt was visiting at the time, he stayed on. Walt was no older than Dave and we all got along very well.

Wanting to impress Walt with my cooking ability, I baked a cake but I forget to put the egg in until the cake was half-baked. I pulled the cake out, mixed the egg in, and returned the pan to the oven. It didn't turn out very well with lumps and egg white all over the top, but they ate it anyway. I made pancakes, eggs and bacon for breakfast and was astounded when Walt ate 12 pancakes, a half- pound of bacon and four eggs. He didn't have an ounce of fat on him and I couldn't believe that he could put away that much food. It was fun having the house all to ourselves and we laughed, played cards and romped around the hills through the whole break. It was a short break but I enjoyed every day of it before I headed back to Palmer for the rest of the school year.

After my great grandparents moved to Anchorage — Fourth Avenue in 1928.

By May, kids chomped at the bit to have school finished and get on to summer. I felt the excitement in the air with each passing day as kids talked about their fun summer plans with the other classmates. That old nagging feeling of aloneness crept over me. I felt torn between two worlds again. I loved the homestead, but I loved being around people as well. As things ended for the school year, The Citizen's Park Committee put on a contest for all the Palmer school kids to name the Palmer City Park. They picked my name for moose Deniigi. The sound is like Den eck ee. It was an Athabaskan Native word meaning moose and since there were so many moose in Palmer, the name fit. I received a $20 savings bond from the Mat-Su Valley Bank. There was supposed to be a ribbon cutting ceremony at the park for me, but it rained and the ceremony never took place. Unfortunately, no one in Palmer knew how to pronounce the name and people came to know the park as Den-ah-kay. The pronunciation didn't really matter though, because the park system failed to put the meaning on the park sign and no one had a clue that it meant moose. Years later, the city sold the property and now there are buildings on the site.

Mom wrote to tell me that Dad had decided to mate Danger to Winnie Pooh and Nikka to build up his dog team. Danger didn't seem interested in either dog and Dad gave up on him. He borrowed one of the Nicklie dogs to do the deed but didn't think that dog was interested either. Dad gave up too early on Danger since he mated with both dogs. Afterward, Winnie Pooh became very possessive of him and pined in the house because she wanted to see him. She fought with Nikka for Danger's attention. Both dogs had pups. Nikka's pups were named Katchie, Kemo, and Pepper and Winnie Pooh's pups were Blueberry and Panda. Dad finally had his dog team.

Mel, the man Dad talked into homesteading the other side of the lake lived in his trailer that winter. In January, he told Mom and Dad that he had ordered a rototilling disc, which they could borrow when it came in the spring. It never came. Dad made plans to rent one from Eagle River, a community twelve miles from Anchorage. The owner freighted the tiller up on the train. To fulfill the requirements of homesteading, a person had to plant a required number of acres in crops on their property and since Dad couldn't afford to buy a tiller, he felt fortunate to find one he could rent. He planted barley and then watched anxiously for it to grow. There were long hours of hot summer sun in Alaska, but it wasn't a long enough period for barley. It grew to 2-1/2 inches and froze in the fall. Mom and Dad were heartbroken. They were so excited about the prospect of growing something.

The Park hired Dave back as the manager for the McKinley Park Service Station. He worked twelve hours a day and six days a week. For all of his responsibility and work he received $350 a month plus room and board.

I also went back to work at the hotel. Instead of working as a maid though, I worked as a waitress in the dining room. The lessons began when the new dining- room manager arrived. She taught us how to carry trays, which side to serve from, how to take the orders, etc. She didn't hold back and yelled at the waitresses in front of the patrons. Since I was shy to begin with, I died a silent death every time her dark eyes rested on me from across the room. One evening I served soup to a couple when she came rushing up to chide me for serving it on the wrong side. The couple felt sorry for me and told me what they thought of her after she walked away. They said it loud enough for her to hear and I scurried away not wanting to her to think that I promoted it. Two weeks after coming, she died in her sleep from a heart condition.

Working in the dining room was not something I enjoyed. I asked Mr. Vaughn if there was any other job opening. He gave me a job taking care of the employee's dining room. I loved it. I helped cook breakfast, served three meals a day to the employees, kept the dining room clean and helped make box lunches for the tourists to take with them on the early morning departures into the park. I scrubbed the dining room floor on my hands and knees and kept the floors waxed to a high polish and Mr. Vaughn was impressed. That much work wasn't required for the job, but I wanted him to be happy with my work. He had become friends with my parents and I not only wanted to please him but my parents as well.

At the beginning of the summer, I hung out in the hotel on my off hours but after being around the college kids, who loved to have fun, I found it more fun to hang out with the party kids. There were the 'party kids' and the 'let's go camping, hiking, ride the bus kids.' I had enough outdoor life on the homestead and didn't care for the ride into the park since I had done it so many times as a young girl that I opted for the party kids. They drove to Cantwell after work and partied. The bar never asked anyone's ages and the college kids partied. I didn't care for the taste of alcohol and knew I would be in big trouble with my parents if anyone saw me drinking. I ordered coke and watched everyone else. We all laughed and had a good time but we went too often and returned to the hotel too late. When we returned around 1 AM and then had to get up at 4 AM, it took its toll. I was so sleep deprived; I had red spots around my eyes. The smell of morning bacon made me nauseous just because I was so sleepy. I put the loaded rashers of bacon and giant pans of eggs in the ovens and stirred the eggs every morning and some mornings it was all I could do to make it through the breakfast. Knowing how I felt after those late night runs Jim, a friend of mine, put a glass of tomato juice and an aspirin on the stair rail for me. It helped with the headache I always had in the morning. After a month of having all that fun, I decided my sleep was more important and I didn't go as often. It was a little lonesome staying behind in an empty dorm though and there wasn't anything to do in the hotel unless there was a movie.

After one of our late night excursions to Cantwell, we girls all went upstairs to our rooms and the boys went to their rooms downstairs. Screams erupted down the hall, and two half-clad girls rushed from their room. They screamed that their room was haunted and stood crying hysterically in the middle of the hall. Suddenly, two more girls raced from their room crying and screaming. Back and forth, all of us ran like a herd of cattle from one end of the hall to the other. It was like being in an earthquake and not knowing where to go for safety. One of the girls screamed, "The mattresses on our beds are flopping up and down!" A few disbelieving girls crept into the two rooms to check it out for themselves and came rushing out screaming when they did indeed see the mattresses jumping on the cots. They even ventured in to look under the beds thinking that someone might be under them. It was dark and bare. Finally, after about thirty minutes of this full- blown hysteria, a girl dropped to her knees beside one of the beds and stayed put. Up came a broom handle through a small hole in the floor and the mattress bounced again. Two of the boys on the bottom floor spent the evening drilling holes through the hardwood floors and through the downstairs ceiling to pull off their little prank. A boy stationed in each of the two rooms poked his broomstick up through the holes. After everyone settled down and stopped shaking, we laughed and laughed over the great joke. Unfortunately, for the boys, it didn't turn out so well. I don't know if they received any jail time for it, but they lost their jobs and were banned from the park.

As I walked on the boardwalk from the dorm to the hotel one evening, I caught a movement out of the corner of my eye. Abreast of the garbage barrel, I turned and saw a grizzly bear on the other side of the barrel. He pulled his head out of the barrel and made a half growl, half grunt sound. I looked right into this bear's beady eyes. With only one bear- sized step between us, I didn't know what he would do. My

A grizzly who doesn't want to be bothered.

mind raced as I tried to figure out whether to go toward the hotel or back toward the dorm, or stand there in hopes that he would leave. The experts say, "Don't run!" but when the heart is pumping blood to the head and the adrenaline rush is on, it's hard not to run. I ran. First, I ran to the back door of the employee's dining room, only to find it locked. I didn't look back to see if the bear was breathing down my neck. I ran around the building to the back entrance of the hotel and ran inside. Then, totally out of breath, and my head pounding with blood, I turned to see if the bear was peering at me through the glass door. When I opened the door and looked down the boardwalk, he was nowhere in sight. I stepped out the door and peered around the corner. There he was contentedly eating garbage out of the garbage can. He hadn't given me a second thought. There were several times when the hotel relocated garbage-eating bears from the hotel area.

I made it home a few times that summer and on one of those occasions, someone knocked on our door. The man asked if he and his family might set up their tent in our field beside the house. Then he asked if he might use our bathroom. Over the years, this happened quite a few times in the summer. City people wanted to get away on a great adventure but were afraid to get too far away from people. We were two and a half miles out of Cantwell with no one past us for seventy miles. I didn't understand why people left the city if they didn't really want an outdoor experience away from people.

At the end of the summer, Dave received a letter from Mr. Vaughn stating that the station made $4,300 more that summer even though there were fewer gas customers. He said that Dave had been a very good manager and he would love to have him back in the future. I also received an invite back.

CHAPTER 10

1963

fall to fall

WHEN I WENT BACK TO PALMER FOR MY SENIOR YEAR THAT FALL, I boarded with Mrs. Trowbridge, the secretary of our high school. As much as I loved my grandparents, I didn't want to stay with them again. They were too far out of Palmer, and I, being involved with school activities, found it hard to get a seven mile ride to my grandparents house after my extracurricular activities. My mother didn't want to inconvenience my stepmother again because she had three girls and the house was too crowded. As a last resort, the school secretary, hearing that I needed a place to live, said I could live with her. Again with Mrs. Trowbridge, it was time to acclimate to new house rules. I was very good at this since I had lived with my grandparents, my aunt, the California couple and my stepmother. With Mrs. Trowbridge, it was about taking a shower every morning. I didn't mind taking showers every day, but I preferred taking them in the evening because the house was freezing in the morning. She turned the house heat down at night and the linoleum floors were like walking on ice. It reminded me of the cement floor in the shower at the homestead. If I had had slippers, it wouldn't have even been an issue but I didn't. I was a guest in her house and I never talked to her about my disliking morning showers since it seemed important to her. It seems like such an inconsequential thing to remember but people do remember weird things from their past. Aside from the morning showers, she let me do my own thing. At this age, I knew my parents rules. Living with her did give me more freedom then I had ever had but I didn't abuse the privilege.

She bowled several nights a week and stayed after school every day so we didn't see much of each other. When she was home, the house was quiet because she normally didn't turn on the TV or radio. When the TV was on sometimes in the evening, we sat in silence. She didn't talk much and we lived in the house without much interaction.

Mom wrote that Dave went to work for Mullen Construction on the Parks Highway and he worked with dynamite. He worked thirteen hours a day, seven days a week as a driller. He drilled holes with a jackhammer and then put dynamite in the holes. Dave wanted to make all the money he could to buy a VW and return to college. It worried me that he might be so tired from all of his hours that he would have an accident with the dynamite. Mom also wrote that Dad was guiding again and gone for a month. She was alone at the homestead and I knew how much she hated that. I loved getting the newsy letters from her but I also worried when the family was so spread out.

I kept myself busy with the drum corp again that year. I also joined the choir, the Triple Trio Singers, and the school newspaper staff as the feature editor.

In Cantwell, Mom drove the school bus all the time now and when a major storm hit, she could only drive 5 mph. It reminded me of when I had to walk in front of the bus in whiteouts.

Dad acquired a standard poodle they named Sugar and now they had more than enough dogs for a whole dog team. I couldn't wait to get home and run them.

I cleaned houses but decided it didn't pay enough and then I took a job at the Frontier Café in Palmer on weekends. I had the graveyard shift even though I wasn't a night person. Nights dragged on with mostly teenagers coming in. Boys stacked sugar cubes on the tables and put my tip under upside down glasses of water and I wasn't amused but they stayed late to keep me company and then the messes I cleaned up didn't seem quite as bad.

Dad trying out two of the sled dogs

Sugar, our Standard Poodle, and another little dog we had for a short time, sitting on our dog sled

The cranky cook threw a pan at me when people sent their eggs back because they weren't cooked enough. He yelled about everything and I dreaded having to go into the kitchen for anything. I had no choice since I also washed the dishes. I dragged myself home in the morning, and fell into bed where I slept the whole day. Burned out after several months, I quit. I decided that housecleaning wasn't so bad after all.

On the homestead, Dad finished the floor in the middle room (our new living room) with plywood, put new Mylar up for the windows and moved a big oil stove into the room. He also put building paper on the ceiling of the bedroom. He opened up the area from the living room into the kitchen by cutting out a section of the wall. Then he put in a few steps going down into the kitchen. They no longer needed a door into the kitchen from the living room area.

Our underground living room with half of the left side and the front out of the ground.

In November, Dad and Mom built all the furniture for the new living room from bridge timbers. Dad built a massive bridge timber coffee table with legs and Mom gave it nine coats of varnish. Dad built the couches into the wall with bridge timbers and Mom made bottom cushions and throw pillows for them. He built in end tables at the end of the couches. The ceiling still had the shiny insulation foil on it but the room was a dream come true and I couldn't wait to go home and see it. Mom made the curtains for the windows and set about decorating. Now I had an established place to sleep when I went home. It was on the bridge timber couch under the plastic Mylar windows. This location was a mixed blessing. When the wind blew, I awoke from the rattling of the plastic. Dad put Mylar on the outside and inside of the frame to create an air space. This insulated the inside from the extreme cold on the outside. When the plastic rattled, it sounded like someone snapping a piece of material back and forth. Some nights I lay staring out the window into the dark abyss for hours, but some nights when I lay there in the silence, I had the awesome thrill of watching the northern lights dance across the sky. The yellowish green and sometimes lavender ribbons shot back and forth, up and down. They danced around like children on a gigantic playground. Eskimos called the lights torches marking the way to heaven for departed souls. Alaskans "oohed" and "ahhed" over the northern lights like people at a fourth of July fireworks display. It wasn't just the northern lights and wind blowing the plastic windows that kept me awake though. Some nights the howling wolves kept me awake. It seemed like the wolves howled more on the nights with no wind and a full moon. The howling had a mournful sound that went on for hours. Sometimes when they howled, our dogs howled from their enclosure.

Right after I learned of all the changes to the house, Mom wrote that when Dad worked on the bus, it fell on him and trapped him under the wheel. Mel heard Mom screaming from across the lake and ran over the ice to help. He called his son, Jim and he flew Dad into the Fairbanks hospital. He wasn't hurt too bad and didn't have to stay in Fairbanks long.

Bill and I started dating again after his return from the Army so when Christmas came I asked my parents if I could bring him home for part of the Christmas break. They said yes and on our train ride to Cantwell I filled his head with wild stories of how we lived. This was my test for him. I thought that any man worth having had to be able to chop wood, fix machinery and know carpentry. I teased him with stories of how we had a door- frame with only a tarp over it and that we used an outhouse. He believed everything I told him. By the time we reached Cantwell, he appeared apprehensive and maybe deep down wanted to go home. I laughed when we got to the front door and saw the expression on his face as he stared at the tarp less door. His first test of worthiness came when I asked him to fill the lanterns and pump them up so I could light them. It wasn't a fair test but he passed. His stay wasn't long before he left on the train and I picked up homestead life again.

The cache and dog enclosure in the background.

I took the dog team down for the mail every day and took them for short trips all over the countryside. As I walked out to their enclosure, the dogs barked and jumped at the fence. They loved getting out and running. They yawned, jumped and ran in circles as I entered their enclosure. I was relieved that Dad never chained his dogs. They were free to run in their enclosure. He kept the dogs in a fenced enclosure around the old goat house. They could go into the goat house to stay warm but he partitioned it off to separate the dogs inside and outside. If they had been on chains, they would have been wolf dinners.

Before each run, I took two dogs out at a time to harness and in their excitement, they tangled themselves in the harnesses. After I had them all ready, they strained at the lead line, anxious to go. We always took off with a jerk which about knocked me off at the start. Nikka, the lead dog, did pretty much what she wanted. If nothing was going on around us, she obeyed my commands but if we saw an animal, she had selective hearing. Some days she did what I wanted and other days, she did what she wanted. One day we saw a herd of caribou and she took off after them, pulling the other dogs along.

I held on and yelled, "Whoa, stop!" No such luck.

I bounced off after a harrowing ride standing on the back brake of the sled and the team continued on, chasing the herd. Fortunately, one of the local men found them tangled in the brush and brought them home. Winnie wasn't commanding enough to make a good leader and the only other possibility for a leader was Sugar, the standard poodle. She was smart and she didn't fight with the other dogs. The only drawback to Sugar was that her paws chunked up with snow. It didn't seem to bother her until the end of the run. Nikka, who had wolf in her, couldn't even get along with her own pups. They even fought through the fence from one enclosure to the next and when they did, they caught their teeth in the fence and bled all over. There was always blood on the fencing wire from their fights. Sugar wasn't a part of it since we kept her in the house most of the time. Her sweet nature was nothing like Nikka's, but I liked Nikka anyway. I spent most of the remainder of my break running the dogs and then it was time to head back to Palmer and school.

When the 1964 earthquake hit with a magnitude of 9.2, I was home alone. It was the largest quake in North America and the second largest ever recorded in the world at that time. I felt a trembling and heard a rumble and then everything shook in the house. At first, I thought a road grader was pushing on the house but that didn't make sense. I then thought that Russia had bombed us or that the end of the world had come. I ran to the window and saw birch trees swaying from side to side. I saw the neighbor's car rolling back and forth in their driveway. The chandelier swung from one side of the ceiling to the other

This is what the roads looked like out of Palmer after the 1964 earthquake.

Downtown Anchorage after the quake.

More of Anchorage after the quake.

and books fell off the shelves. Figurines from the shelves broke into pieces on the floor. Then the refrigerator door flew open and the contents hurled across the kitchen floor. I ran to the doorway and held on to the door frame stabilizing myself. As I looked at the neighbor's house, I watched as their brick chimney fell off the house. My shaking legs barely held me up and when the earthquake stopped, I ran for the phone to call Bill. He came on the heels of Mrs. Trowbridge and asked if I wanted to drive downtown with him to see the aftermath. We were shocked. All of the liquor bottles had broken at the liquor store and booze flowed out the door and down the sidewalk into the gutter. Every knickknack fell off the shelves and now lay in broken pieces in the aisles at one of the local stores. Roads were riddled with massive cracks running down the middle and on the shoulders, and the railroad track slid off its pad like icing sliding off a cake. There was an eerie silence as we drove down the streets with our windows down. Bill took me home after a few hours of viewing the destruction. As the evening wore on and we waited for aftershocks, I, too tired to stay awake any longer, went to bed. Mrs. Trowbridge lay down on the couch fully dressed, ready to run from the house. Small tremors shook me from my sleep all night.

People called their families and friends until all the lines overloaded and jammed. I couldn't get through to my brother in Anchorage but when I finally heard from him, he had a scarier story than mine. He and a friend had rented an apartment in a high-rise apartment building. They left their suitcases in the apartment with plans to finish moving in that evening. That building collapsed to the ground in the quake. He felt fortunate that he was not at the apartment when it went down. He worked at a car parts store on Fifth Avenue and when the shaking started, he and other employees ran from the store. As a pole crashed down, Dave pulled one of the female employees out of the way. He saved her life and they married one and a half years later. He took pictures of the aftermath in Anchorage with its sunken streets and leveled buildings. His friends told him of their harrowing experiences when they tried driving down streets as crevasses opened. Some cars were abandoned because there was no safe street to drive on and others fell into the open cracks in the streets but managed to crawl out. In Turnagain Arms (a bay view area of Anchorage), one family ran from their house to the end of their concrete walkway when their little girl ran back for their dog. The earth opened up as she reached the house and she and the house fell in. The crack closed and in an instant, she disappeared as her family stood there in shock.

Mom called from Cantwell and said the house creaked and groaned when the earthquake hit. They ran outside and the lake made noises. They didn't know what to do because they didn't know what was happening. They were 210 miles from Anchorage.

The kids were full of energy and excitement at school on Monday and they all had their own horror stories.

Somewhere along the way, Bill and I stopped seeing each other. I guess the relationship ran its course. I think my brother had something to do with my moving on because he kept saying, "If you marry a local Palmer boy, he will never leave Palmer and you'll end up with a bunch of kids and never see anything of the world." I wanted to travel and see the world and I felt that he might be right.

Mom wrote that the store owner, Lloyd Davis, sold the Cantwell store and property to Al Smith and family in April. She also told me to call the store at 4:30 PM on Wednesday or Saturday if I ever wanted to get ahold of her because those were the only days she picked up mail. Not getting to talk to her at times was hard because when I had a problem in my life, I had to work it out on my own. A public phone was not conducive to a good heartfelt talk. At the end of her letter, she said that someone left a trailer at their place so now I would have a place of my own to sleep in.

When I graduated that year, my brother threw a small graduation party for me with his friends and a few days later, he saw me off at the train station as I headed back to Cantwell.

It was a beautiful spring and I had some time off before I went to work at the park hotel again. I decided to go camping up the railroad tracks. Mom thought I was too young to go off on my own at seventeen but I assured her that if I took Nikka and a 22 rifle, I would be fine. I didn't know where to go when I boarded the train, but when the north bound train pulled into Nenana, I decided to get off. I ran to the cargo car for my pack and Nikka and taking her out of their cage, we disembarked. It was intimidating getting off in a town I didn't know and I wondered if I had chosen the right stop as I walked to the outskirts of town and set up my tent. People eyed me suspiciously as I walked through town and right after I set up my tent, a young man came to tell me that the minister wanted me to give up my rifle while there. I hated being without a gun but I didn't think I had a choice and I gave the man my rifle. He assured me that I could pick it up at the minister's house on my way out of town. I didn't have any agenda so I walked back into town with Nikka and tied her up outside of the local café, I ventured in to have a hamburger and ordered one for her. The woman gave me a look of disdain when I said I wanted a hamburger for my dog. She served me and made it plain that she wasn't interested in conversation even though there wasn't another sole in the café. I took the hint and ate in silence. Nikka loved her hamburger and was interested in sniffing everything we passed on our way back to the tent.

Nenana was another community steeped in history. It sat at the confluence of the Tanana River and Nenana River. Boats and barges ferried supplies to the Interior villages. Nenana was the gateway to the Interior.

My first night in Nenana frightened me. I found myself waking up with every sound. Every time Nikka sat up and raised her ears, I sat up and strained to hear what she heard.

The second day, I took a ferry ride on the stern wheeler that crossed the Nenana River. It was the only way to get to Fairbanks from Nenana since no bridge existed across the wide river. In the winter, people drove across the frozen river but in the summer, the ferry connected the small town to Fairbanks. This ferry traversed the river with a chain driven diesel paddle wheel. A man named George Black out of Fairbanks built the ferry and named it *The Idler*. In the beginning, the owner utilized the ferry for the mail route but when Mr. Black drown, his son-in-law,

The Nenana stern wheeler.

Art Peterson, took over and renamed it the *Yutana Barge Line* for the Yukon and Tanana Rivers. Art later sold it to Mr. Binkley and through its long history, the ferry only travelled across the river now. The rivers in Alaska were the roads in the early years of Alaska.

Wherever the Natives roamed, the river names had one thing in common. They all ended in Na ie. Nenana, Tanana, Susitna, Skwentna, Alatna, and Talkeetna. Na in Athabaskan means river and it always struck me as strange to say Nenana River or Tanana River. It's like saying Nenana River River. Every time I crossed one of these rivers and saw the sign, I thought, *redundant.*

The road to Fairbanks started on the other side of the river and with no bridge to cross over the stern wheeler met the needs of the community. Wanting to see everything, I jumped aboard for a fifty- cent ride across. By the time I rode the river in each direction, the captain, Mr. Riley and I were friends. He invited me to ride it again and I did. On the second round trip, I asked him if I might look through the cabins on board and he let me. When I looked in the staterooms on the old stern wheeler, I tried to visualize when they were last used. I could picture someone like my great grandparents riding the stern wheeler down the river. Mr. Riley couldn't help me much as to when the staterooms were used but as we talked the subject came around to how scared I had been the night before. I told him about my having to give up my rifle to the minister and he didn't understand why I had complied. He was upset by such a demand and said he wouldn't mind if I threw my sleeping bag down on the floor of his cabin. I felt comfortable with him so I accepted.

The next day was his day off and he invited me to ride into Fairbanks with him. We left Nikka in an enclosure at the cabin, took the stern wheeler across the river, and got into his pickup on the other side. What an adventure! Being out on my own, doing what I wanted and seeing new things was exhilarating. Fairbanks had changed since I saw it last. There were more people, and the pace had quickened since my first visit. After an exhausting day, we headed back to Nenana before the stern wheeler docked for the night. I spent one more night and then because there wasn't anything else to do in Nenana and Mr. Riley was working, Nikka and I went to the dock to say goodbye, collected my rifle from the minister, and caught the train back to Cantwell. It had been a fun outing.

I left Nikka in Cantwell and Mom drove me to the park hotel to resume the same duties as the summer before.

The monotony of doing the same thing every day grew wearisome and we all tried to find different things to do. I decided to hitchhike from the park to the homestead in Cantwell. It was a thirty- mile stretch on a gravel road. Fayrene, a friend of mine, thought it sounded like fun and said she would go with me. Thirty miles didn't seem like much when we talked about it and I assured her that we would probably get a ride.

We were both off the next day and decided that we would leave after her shift was over at 10 PM. I had to get up at my normal time of 4 AM that day and after my shift, I hung around and waited until ten. When she finished, we made a few sandwiches and headed down the road. During the first few miles, a few cars stopped to offer us a ride but we declined because we had just started and I wanted to walk a little before riding the rest of the way. I reassured Fayrene that there would be many opportunities to ride after we walked a little bit farther. The sun was up all night and it seemed like such an adventure. I carried a heavy pack loaded with Mom's rugs I had washed in the big washers for her. I was sure we would get a ride after our initial offers but after the first few offers, it was late and no one else passed. The mosquitoes were vicious. We didn't have insect repellent and just had to swat them away or take the bite. The grader had graded the gravel road and sharp rocks as well as round rocks twisted under our tennis shoes. It was hard not to twist our ankles. After a few hours of walking, we were both so sleepy from getting up early and being up late that we decided to look for a place to take a nap. I knew there was a small runway down the road called Lingo's Airport so we ventured on. When we reached the airport, we discovered an unlocked trailer on the site and let ourselves in. It was cold outside and even colder in the trailer. Even though it was light outside, it chilled off in the evenings. We unloaded the rugs, laid them on the floor to sleep on, and covered ourselves with some discarded newspapers but trying to sleep on a cold, hard floor wasn't restful and after a few hours we got up. We loaded the rugs into my pack and moved on. The sun had finally warmed our chilled bodies and we decided to stop and eat our sandwiches beside a stream. I needed to soak my now blistered feet. I took my shoes off and put my feet into the icy cold stream water while we ate.

Right after we left the stream and crossed the bridge, we turned to see a huge grizzly bear on the road forty feet from us. There were no tall trees to climb and I, loaded down with rugs, knew I couldn't get up a tree anyway. People always said, "If you are attacked by a bear, roll up into a fetal position, throw your coat over your head and play dead." I can't imagine lying there quietly while a bear gnawed off my leg, although I do know a man who did just that and lived to tell about it. Another man, near Cantwell, lay there while the bear ripped him from head to waist. He put his hat on to hold his head together on his hike out of the brush. He also lived to tell about it. This man survived after hundreds of stitches.

This nine-foot-plus, grizzly bear stood up on his hind legs and sniffed the air for what seemed like an eternity as we stood facing him in frozen silence. The bear finally dropped down on all fours and meandered down the bank beside the bridge. We didn't know whether he would change his mind and come after us as we backed away. After a short distance we turned around and hurried off down the road.

My knee started to throb as the morning wore on. There was excruciating pain with each step. By the time we reached the Nenana No. 1 Bridge, nine miles from the homestead, I had to lean on Fayrene, put my hand behind my knee, and push my leg forward. Cars passed us but no one stopped. We reached the homestead at noon, I had torn the cartilage in my knee, and my feet were bloody with blisters. The rugs and my cheap, ill-fitting, flat, tennis shoes had destroyed me. Our ride back to the park came after we had a short visit with my parents. We had arranged for a friend at the hotel to pick us up for the return since we only had that day off. The nurse at the hotel wrapped my knee and for the next three weeks, I kept my leg elevated and iced down when I wasn't working. I couldn't stay off my feet as I was told because of my job. I limped around the dining room and took care of the leg after work.

Every time I went home, I saw more and more vehicles on our homestead and I knew that they didn't belong to us. Someone had left another small trailer and I saw a pickup as well as two cars. The people leaving these things came to Alaska to work construction for the summer and if their vehicle broke down, they left it at the homestead because Dad was so accommodating. If an axle broke on their summer trailer that they had hauled up the Alcan Highway, they asked if they could leave it for a while. Their intentions were to return the following summer and retrieve the items, but due to finances, lack of an Alaska summer job, or not wanting to put the money into the repairs, they never returned. Soon, the homestead looked like a wrecking yard and Mom hated it. There weren't just vehicles from other people but from Dad as well. He had old trucks and cars for parts. One day she put her foot down and said that Dad had to find a spot in the trees at the end of the homestead and hide all of the vehicles. We named the spot our 'bone yard.' When company came and we talked of having things down at the 'bone yard', their eyes were the size of saucers. If someone needed parts for something, they could find it in Everett's 'bone yard.' As long as the vehicles were out of Mom's sight, she accepted their existence.

At the end of the summer, I went to the employee's Christmas party. All of the employees made presents for the person whose name they drew or they purchased a gift for under $5. It was fun seeing what people made for each other. My present that summer was a wooden apple the cook carved for me with a note wishing me success in college. I applied and was accepted to Central Washington State College in Ellensburg, Washington.

CHAPTER 11

1964

fall to fall

WHEN I ARRIVED IN ELLENSBURG, WASHINGTON FOR COLLEGE, I WAS impressed with the beauty of the college. Beautiful ivy grew up the sides of all the brick buildings and everything was green. I picked up papers for my classes, found an apartment since the dorms were full, and found a job in short order. I actually found two jobs. One was selling dining out cards over the phone and the other was working at a bus station in the café. I had three roommates and two bedrooms with one bed in one and two in the other. We rotated periodically since one person had to sleep on the couch.

Everything was different but exciting at college. When the other kids wrote their essays for English class, they wrote about things they did that summer. My essays were about riding on my first escalator or riding in an elevator. I wrote about the time I came out of the grocery store with my arms full and the door opened. I turned to thank someone but no one was there. It was my first experience with automatic doors.

I befriended a young man named Jack who couldn't get enough of my talk about Alaska and its beauty. Every time I saw him, he asked for more stories about the last frontier. He ended up going to Alaska after he left college and I saw him several times in Anchorage. Unfortunately, he flew with a friend one day when another plane, not seeing them, came down on top of them and drove them into the ground. Small planes are abundant in Alaska and as a result, there are plane crashes every year.

In November, I received a letter from Mom. She wrote that they had a new light plant and could now play the phonograph as much as they liked. They also used a toaster and iron. I thought about the toaster we had when I grew up. It was a four-sided open tin contraption with holes in it and sat over the propane stove burner my parents now had. The toast usually burned. I also thought about how easy it was to use an electric iron versus a flat stove iron or kerosene iron. They also had a phone line from the homestead to Mel, the neighbor across the lake. Mom said it felt good having a connection to someone. She went on to say, "Dad was dragged for quite a distance when the dog team saw a caribou. He ached all over the next day." I sure knew about being along for a ride on the dog sled. I was more fortunate for having been bounced off.

When Mom wrote again, it was to tell me that the wolves killed Sugar, our Standard Poodle. She and Blueberry went for a little romp over the hill while Dad worked outside. When he looked up and saw Blueberry running toward him, scared to death, Dad knew something was wrong. When Sugar didn't return, Dad strapped on his snowshoes and went looking for her. Not far from the house, he found her tracks mixed in with the tracks of five wolves. Then he found a bloody patch and some of Sugar's hair. A wolf drew Sugar into the pack by going up to her alone and leading her back to the pack. She was a friendly dog and probably thought they were friendly dogs. They all closed in on her and tore her apart. They ate every bit of her. Visualizing her end was a gruesome picture that no dog deserves. This gentle, sweet dog hadn't been like any of the other fighting sled dogs. A friend of Mom and Dads' felt so bad about Sugar that he gave them a small black poodle named Keiki. The dog certainly wasn't sledding material, but he brought some comfort.

School and work were a blur. Tired so much of the time from getting off at midnight from the bus stop, I sat at the kitchen table studying and drinking cold coffee. Not because I liked cold coffee but because it always cooled off before I remembered to drink it. Sometimes, I just sat, too tired to think or study. I zoned out and thought about Alaska.

One day, I remembered Grandma telling me how Great Grandma used to clean her hair. I decided to try it. I bought a box of cornstarch and sprinkled half the box on my head. My hair turned white and I couldn't get it out so I washed it in hot water. Then my head gummed up like gravy and I couldn't get it out. When I called Grandma, she said, "Oh, no. I didn't say cornstarch. I said she rubbed cornmeal into her hair and it left it silky and shiny." I guess I wasn't such a good listener.

After finishing college that year, I flew back to Anchorage and took the train back to Cantwell for a short visit with my parents. I decided that as much as I hated leaving the homestead and Cantwell, it was time to move on and find a job in Anchorage. Little did I know that I would be drawn back to the homestead for the rest of my life.

Epilogue

This is the homestead house at the end of Dad's building days. It was never completed on the upper part.

IN THE YEARS AFTER I LEFT THE HOMESTEAD, DAD BOUGHT A windmill for power. Then he built an underground greenhouse with only the south side and roof sticking out of the sand. He hand- built

The summer view behind our cabin

solar panels on top and piped in hot water under the sand in the greenhouse for heat. The water was heated with a small wood/coal stove. He then dug another tunnel connecting the underground kitchen to the greenhouse. In the winter, he had cucumbers, tomatoes, peppers, squash, herbs, flowers, lettuce, beets and dill.

There were hardships on the homestead over the years. One summer a bear came through the property and disemboweled one of the goats in the goat yard. The bear didn't eat the goat. He just killed it. Dad then built a place back into the sand bank for the goats to stay out of the weather. Wire fence surrounded the small goat enclosure but as the wolves grew bolder, Dad had to put barbed wire over the top of the enclosure to keep the wolves from jumping the fence and killing the goats. He ran the barbed wire back and forth over the top of the enclosure to keep the wolves from standing on it or getting through. The wolves stood on top of the sand dome covering the goats' underground den but they couldn't get to the goats. My brother John (Charlie) lost all but two of his sled dogs when wolves closed in on the area where he kept his dogs chained next to their doghouses. Dad had never chained his dogs but he didn't want John's dogs by the house and John was forced to chain them across the road. For several nights, the dogs were agitated and barked but John had no idea why. The wolves must have been stalking the dog area. The day the wolves closed in, several of the dogs broke their chains and ran away from the homestead. Wolves chased them down and killed them. The two dogs who cowered in their dog houses lived. Locals surmised that the wolves wouldn't venture into the dog area to kill them. Only the runners died. John gave one of the survivors away and kept the other survivor, Dawson, to live to a ripe old age. People in the bush of Alaska accept their hardships even though they seem overwhelming at times. I look back on some of the homestead events as tragic but the rest are fond memories.

I loved my years in Cantwell in a closed community. The only road in closed in the winter and the train only ran a few times a week. There was a strong sense of community. No bullying took place like I saw in the larger schools. In those days, we were like one big family. People

In the misty morning behind the cabin.

helped each other whether it was to pull someone out of a ditch or help someone fix broken equipment.

Even after I moved to Anchorage to be a flight attendant for Cordova Airlines and then moved on to work for oil companies, I continued going back home to Cantwell. Things slowed down for me when I returned.

When the state discovered that my parents had short-changed themselves on their allowable homestead property, they were given the opportunity to choose twenty more acres. I rooted for Ice Box Canyon because of my childhood memories, but my parents chose a piece across the graveled Denali Highway. There were more trees on that side as well as a stream. Mom talked Dad into giving me acreage on the homestead property on my twenty-first birthday and I had my pick of any place on that twenty acres. Dad showed me a spot he liked but it wasn't my choice because the view ended at the trees. I ultimately picked a spot with a view to the east. The view went on and on with a slough winding its way back to a lake. Groupings of trees sprinkled the view from my spot all the way past the back lake and on to a mountain range several miles away.

Sunrises and sunsets filled the sky with brilliant oranges. Eerie fog shrouded the slough early in the morning and there were double rainbows after a rain. The view was then and still is spectacular.

By twenty-four, I had enough money saved to build a pre-cut cabin and I did just that. With my brother, Dad, and our friend, Walt, we put up the framework in three days and I finished it over the winter. After that, I lived in my cabin for six months to enjoy the fruits of my labor. Electricity came to Cantwell in the 1980s, which made it easier for everyone. I enjoyed the peacefulness of my setting and loved my animal visitors.

Ducks and trumpeter swans flew in to have their babies each summer and moose ate the vegetation off the slough bottom. The water rose with the rain and sometimes turned the slough into a lake. Mountains reflected in the still water and I never tired of looking out my windows. Different birds sang into the night with the sun shining all night. In

A black bear with an attitude.

A bear in the park rolling in the first big snow.